FINANCIAL ACCOUNTING FOR BEGINNERS

Easy Guide to Financial Statements, Basics & Real-World Examples

ANGELITA RODRIGUEZ B

Copyright Page

This book is provided for informational and educational purposes only. The author and publisher have made every effort to ensure the accuracy of the information presented at the time of publication. However, no guarantee is given regarding the completeness, accuracy, or applicability of the content to individual situations.

Financial practices, accounting standards, and tax regulations vary across countries and jurisdictions and may change over time. Readers are encouraged to consult qualified financial professionals, accountants, or tax advisors for guidance specific to their circumstances.

Disclaimer

The information contained in this book is intended to provide a clear introduction to financial accounting concepts and practices. It is not intended to serve as legal, financial, tax, or professional advice.

While accounting principles follow certain universal standards, financial laws, reporting requirements, and tax obligations can vary significantly depending on location, industry, and individual circumstances. Readers should always verify applicable regulations and seek professional advice when making financial or business decisions.

The examples and scenarios used throughout this book are simplified for educational purposes. They are designed to illustrate accounting concepts rather than represent complete financial or tax guidance.

By reading this book, you acknowledge that the author and publisher are not responsible for any actions taken based on the information presented.

Preface

Many people encounter accounting for the first time and feel an immediate sense of distance from the subject. The terminology seems unfamiliar. Financial statements appear dense and technical. Even simple reports can feel intimidating when the language is new.

Yet accounting itself is not as complicated as it first appears.

At its core, accounting is simply a structured way of understanding how money moves through a business. It records what comes in, what goes out, what a business owns, and what it owes. When these pieces are organized properly, they reveal patterns that help people understand whether a business is healthy, struggling, growing, or drifting in the wrong direction.

The challenge is that many introductions to accounting focus too heavily on terminology and formal rules before readers have had time to see the bigger picture. As a result, beginners sometimes feel like they are memorizing procedures without understanding why those procedures matter.

This book was written to approach the subject differently.

Instead of presenting accounting as a set of complicated technical requirements, the goal here is to explain it as a logical system—one that anyone can learn to understand with the right guidance. Each idea builds gradually on the previous one, moving from basic concepts toward practical financial interpretation.

The focus throughout the book is clarity. Concepts are explained using straightforward language, familiar situations, and examples that reflect how businesses actually operate. Rather than overwhelming readers with unnecessary detail, the emphasis remains on the core principles that make accounting useful in everyday decisions.

Whether you are a student encountering accounting for the first time, a small business owner trying to understand your financial reports, a freelancer managing your own income and expenses, or a professional who simply wants greater financial awareness, the goal is the same: to make the numbers understandable.

Once the structure behind financial statements becomes clear, accounting stops feeling like a foreign language. It becomes a practical tool—one that helps you see what is happening inside a business and make better decisions because of it.

About the Author

Angelita Rodriguez B writes practical guides designed to make complex topics easier to understand. With a focus on clarity and real-world application, their work helps readers build confidence in areas that often seem intimidating at first.

Through straightforward explanations and practical examples, Angelita Rodriguez B aims to bridge the gap between technical knowledge and everyday understanding. Their writing focuses on helping beginners develop useful skills that can be applied in education, business, and personal financial decision-making.

Financial literacy plays an important role in modern life, and clear explanations can make that knowledge accessible to a wider audience. Books like this are written with that goal in mind—turning complicated subjects into tools that readers can actually use.

TABLE OF CONTENTS

Copyright Page ....

Disclaimer ....

Preface ....

About the Author ....

CHAPTER 1 ....

WHY FINANCIAL ACCOUNTING MATTERS ....

What Financial Accounting Really Is ....

Accounting vs. Bookkeeping vs. Finance ....

Why Businesses Depend on Accounting ....

Real-World Situations Where Accounting Knowledge Matters ....

CHAPTER 2 ....

HOW MONEY FLOWS THROUGH A BUSINESS ....

UNDERSTANDING REVENUE AND EXPENSES ....

ASSETS, LIABILITIES, AND EQUITY IN SIMPLE TERMS ....

HOW BUSINESSES TRACK INCOME AND COSTS ....

THE FINANCIAL LIFE CYCLE OF A BUSINESS ....

WHY EVERY TRANSACTION MATTERS ....

CHAPTER 3 ....

THE LANGUAGE OF ACCOUNTING ....

ESSENTIAL ACCOUNTING TERMS EVERY BEGINNER SHOULD KNOW ....

REVENUE, EXPENSES, AND PROFIT EXPLAINED ....

CAPITAL, INVESTMENTS, AND OWNER'S EQUITY ....
UNDERSTANDING FINANCIAL TRANSACTIONS ....
COMMON ACCOUNTING TERMS USED IN BUSINESS REPORTS ....
CHAPTER 4 ....
THE ACCOUNTING EQUATION ....
THE FOUNDATION OF FINANCIAL ACCOUNTING ....
UNDERSTANDING ASSETS = LIABILITIES + EQUITY ....
HOW TRANSACTIONS AFFECT THE ACCOUNTING EQUATION ....
SIMPLE EXAMPLES OF THE ACCOUNTING EQUATION IN ACTION ....
WHY THE ACCOUNTING EQUATION ALWAYS BALANCES ....
CHAPTER 5 ....
THE DOUBLE-ENTRY ACCOUNTING SYSTEM ....
WHY ACCOUNTING USES TWO ENTRIES FOR EVERY TRANSACTION ....
UNDERSTANDING DEBITS AND CREDITS ....
HOW ACCOUNTS INCREASE AND DECREASE ....
Assets ....
EXAMPLES OF DOUBLE-ENTRY TRANSACTIONS ....
COMMON BEGINNER MISTAKES WITH DEBITS AND CREDITS ....
CHAPTER 6 ....
RECORDING FINANCIAL TRANSACTIONS ....
WHY RECORDING TRANSACTIONS IS IMPORTANT ....

SOURCE DOCUMENTS AND FINANCIAL RECORDS ....

THE STEPS IN RECORDING TRANSACTIONS ....

INTRODUCTION TO JOURNAL ENTRIES ....

ORGANIZING FINANCIAL INFORMATION ....

CHAPTER 7 ....

THE GENERAL JOURNAL ....

WHAT THE GENERAL JOURNAL IS ....

THE STRUCTURE OF A JOURNAL ENTRY ....

RECORDING TRANSACTIONS STEP-BY-STEP ....

PRACTICAL EXAMPLES OF JOURNAL ENTRIES ....

AVOIDING COMMON JOURNAL ENTRY ERRORS ....

CHAPTER 8 ....

THE GENERAL LEDGER ....

WHAT THE GENERAL LEDGER DOES ....

UNDERSTANDING DIFFERENT TYPES OF ACCOUNTS ....

POSTING JOURNAL ENTRIES TO THE LEDGER ....

TRACKING ACCOUNT BALANCES ....

ORGANIZING FINANCIAL DATA FOR REPORTING ....

CHAPTER 9 ....

TRIAL BALANCE AND ACCURACY ....

WHAT A TRIAL BALANCE IS ....

PREPARING A TRIAL BALANCE ....

WHY TRIAL BALANCES MUST ALWAYS BALANCE ....

IDENTIFYING AND CORRECTING ERRORS ....

THE ROLE OF ACCURACY IN FINANCIAL REPORTING ....

CHAPTER 10
ADJUSTING ENTRIES AND ACCOUNTING PERIODS
WHY ADJUSTMENTS ARE NECESSARY
ACCRUED REVENUES AND EXPENSES
PREPAID EXPENSES AND UNEARNED REVENUE
DEPRECIATION EXPLAINED SIMPLY
PREPARING ACCOUNTS FOR FINANCIAL STATEMENTS
CHAPTER 11
INTRODUCTION TO FINANCIAL STATEMENTS
THE PURPOSE OF FINANCIAL STATEMENTS
THE THREE CORE FINANCIAL REPORTS
HOW FINANCIAL STATEMENTS WORK TOGETHER
WHY BUSINESSES RELY ON FINANCIAL REPORTS
UNDERSTANDING FINANCIAL REPORTING PERIODS
CHAPTER 12
THE INCOME STATEMENT
WHAT THE INCOME STATEMENT SHOWS
REVENUE AND COST OF GOODS SOLD
OPERATING EXPENSES EXPLAINED
CALCULATING PROFIT AND NET INCOME
EXAMPLE OF A SIMPLE INCOME STATEMENT
CHAPTER 13
THE BALANCE SHEET
WHAT THE BALANCE SHEET REVEALS

CURRENT VS. NON-CURRENT ASSETS
UNDERSTANDING LIABILITIES
OWNER'S EQUITY EXPLAINED
EXAMPLE OF A BALANCE SHEET
CHAPTER 14
THE CASH FLOW STATEMENT
WHY CASH FLOW MATTERS
OPERATING ACTIVITIES
INVESTING ACTIVITIES
FINANCING ACTIVITIES
EXAMPLE OF A CASH FLOW STATEMENT
CHAPTER 15
CONNECTING THE FINANCIAL STATEMENTS
HOW THE INCOME STATEMENT AFFECTS THE BALANCE SHEET
HOW CASH FLOW REFLECTS BUSINESS ACTIVITY
UNDERSTANDING THE FINANCIAL STORY OF A BUSINESS
WHY THESE STATEMENTS MUST ALIGN
READING FINANCIAL REPORTS AS A COMPLETE SYSTEM
CHAPTER 16
HOW TO READ FINANCIAL STATEMENTS
IDENTIFYING FINANCIAL STRENGTHS
RECOGNIZING WARNING SIGNS IN FINANCIAL REPORTS
INTERPRETING REVENUE AND PROFIT TRENDS
UNDERSTANDING EXPENSE PATTERNS

USING FINANCIAL STATEMENTS TO ASK BETTER QUESTIONS

CHAPTER 17

BASIC FINANCIAL ANALYSIS

WHY FINANCIAL ANALYSIS MATTERS

PROFITABILITY INDICATORS

LIQUIDITY AND FINANCIAL STABILITY

SIMPLE FINANCIAL RATIOS EXPLAINED

INTERPRETING FINANCIAL PERFORMANCE

CHAPTER 18

PROFIT VS. CASH FLOW

WHY PROFIT DOES NOT ALWAYS MEAN CASH

HOW CASH FLOW AFFECTS BUSINESS SURVIVAL

UNDERSTANDING LIQUIDITY

MANAGING CASH EFFECTIVELY

REAL-WORLD CASH FLOW SCENARIOS

CHAPTER 19

COMMON ACCOUNTING MISTAKES BEGINNERS MAKE

CONFUSING REVENUE WITH PROFIT

MISCLASSIFYING EXPENSES

IGNORING CASH FLOW

POOR RECORD KEEPING

HOW TO AVOID COSTLY ACCOUNTING ERRORS

CHAPTER 20

ACCOUNTING FOR SMALL BUSINESSES

WHY ENTREPRENEURS MUST UNDERSTAND ACCOUNTING

TRACKING REVENUE AND EXPENSES ....
MONITORING PROFITABILITY ....
KEEPING ORGANIZED FINANCIAL RECORDS ....
BUILDING A SIMPLE ACCOUNTING SYSTEM ....
CHAPTER 21 ....
USING ACCOUNTING FOR BETTER DECISIONS ....
FINANCIAL DATA IN BUSINESS DECISIONS ....
BUDGETING BASICS ....
PRICING AND PROFITABILITY ....
EVALUATING BUSINESS GROWTH ....
MANAGING FINANCIAL RISKS ....
CHAPTER 22 ....
UNDERSTANDING FINANCIAL REPORTS AT WORK ....
FINANCIAL REPORTS USED IN COMPANIES ....
HOW MANAGERS USE FINANCIAL DATA ....
PARTICIPATING IN FINANCIAL DISCUSSIONS ....
UNDERSTANDING PERFORMANCE METRICS ....
IMPROVING FINANCIAL AWARENESS IN THE WORKPLACE ....
CHAPTER 23 ....
ACCOUNTING TOOLS AND TECHNOLOGY ....
INTRODUCTION TO ACCOUNTING SOFTWARE ....
DIGITAL BOOKKEEPING SYSTEMS ....
AUTOMATION IN MODERN ACCOUNTING ....
CHOOSING THE RIGHT ACCOUNTING TOOLS ....
USING TECHNOLOGY TO SIMPLIFY FINANCIAL MANAGEMENT ....
CHAPTER 24 ....
ACCOUNTING AND TAXES ....

WHY ACCURATE FINANCIAL RECORDS MATTER FOR TAXES
BASIC FINANCIAL DOCUMENTATION
PREPARING FINANCIAL DATA FOR TAX REPORTING
WORKING WITH ACCOUNTANTS AND TAX PROFESSIONALS
AVOIDING TAX-RELATED FINANCIAL MISTAKES
CHAPTER 25
A COMPLETE ACCOUNTING EXAMPLE
SETTING UP A SIMPLE BUSINESS SCENARIO
RECORDING TRANSACTIONS STEP-BY-STEP
PREPARING FINANCIAL STATEMENTS
Statement of Owner's Equity
Balance Sheet
Simple Cash Flow View
INTERPRETING THE FINANCIAL RESULTS
LESSONS FROM THE EXAMPLE
CHAPTER 26
KEY ACCOUNTING PRINCIPLES TO REMEMBER
CORE ACCOUNTING CONCEPTS RECAP
ESSENTIAL FINANCIAL RULES FOR BEGINNERS
BEST PRACTICES FOR FINANCIAL RECORD KEEPING
BUILDING LONG-TERM FINANCIAL CONFIDENCE
CHAPTER 27
YOUR NEXT STEPS IN FINANCIAL LEARNING
APPLYING ACCOUNTING KNOWLEDGE IN REAL LIFE

CONTINUING YOUR FINANCIAL EDUCATION ....
DEVELOPING FINANCIAL AWARENESS ....
BUILDING CONFIDENCE WITH BUSINESS NUMBERS ....

CHAPTER 1

WHY FINANCIAL ACCOUNTING MATTERS

Financial accounting is often seen as a complicated subject reserved for accountants, auditors, or finance professionals. Many people assume that accounting is filled with complicated formulas, endless calculations, and confusing terminology. In reality, the core purpose of financial accounting is much simpler. It is about **understanding the story behind money**—where it comes from, where it goes, and what it tells us about the health of a business.

Whether someone runs a small business, works in a company, manages freelance income, or studies business in school, financial accounting plays a crucial role in making informed decisions. Without accounting, it would be almost impossible for organizations to understand whether they are making profits, losing money, or managing resources efficiently.

This chapter introduces the foundations of financial accounting and explains why it matters in the real world. Before learning technical concepts like financial statements or journal entries, it is important to understand **what accounting is, how it differs from related fields, and why businesses rely on it every day**.

By the end of this chapter, you will see accounting not as a difficult subject but as a practical tool that helps individuals and businesses make better decisions.

What Financial Accounting Really Is

At its core, financial accounting is the process of **recording, organizing, and communicating financial information about a business.**

Every business activity involves money in some way. A company sells products, pays employees, buys equipment, rents office space, or receives payments from customers. Each of these actions affects the financial position of the business.

Financial accounting tracks these activities and turns them into structured information that can be understood and analyzed.

In simple terms, financial accounting answers questions like:

- How much money did the business earn?
- What expenses did the business incur?
- Does the business own more assets than it owes in debts?
- Is the business financially healthy?

To answer these questions, accounting gathers financial data and summarizes it in standardized reports called **financial statements.**

These statements include:

- The **income statement**, which shows profit or loss
- The **balance sheet**, which shows what the business owns and owes
- The **cash flow statement**, which shows how money moves in and out of the business

Together, these reports provide a clear picture of a company's financial performance and financial position.

Financial accounting is often compared to a **language of business.** Just as language helps people communicate ideas, accounting helps businesses communicate financial information.

For example, imagine an investor considering whether to invest in a company. The investor cannot simply rely on marketing claims or promises. Instead, they need objective financial information. Financial accounting provides that information in a structured and standardized way.

The same principle applies to lenders, managers, employees, and even government regulators. Everyone relies on financial accounting to understand how a business is performing.

Another important feature of financial accounting is that it follows **established rules and standards**. These rules ensure that financial information is consistent, reliable, and comparable across different companies.

Without these standards, one company might report profits in one way while another company reports them differently, making comparison impossible.

Because of this, financial accounting focuses on accuracy, transparency, and consistency.

But perhaps the most important point to remember is this: financial accounting is not just about numbers. It is about **understanding the story those numbers tell about a business**.

When you learn financial accounting, you are learning how to read that story.

Accounting vs. Bookkeeping vs. Finance

People often use the terms **accounting, bookkeeping, and finance** interchangeably. While these fields are related, they are not the same. Understanding the difference helps clarify the role of financial accounting within a business.

Let us start with bookkeeping.

Bookkeeping is the process of **recording financial transactions**. It focuses on capturing daily business activities in an organized way.

Examples of bookkeeping tasks include:

- Recording sales
- Tracking expenses
- Logging payments from customers
- Recording purchases from suppliers
- Maintaining financial records

Think of bookkeeping as the **foundation of the financial record system**. Without accurate bookkeeping, it would be impossible to produce reliable financial reports.

If bookkeeping records the raw data, accounting is the process of **analyzing and interpreting that data.**

Accounting takes the information collected through bookkeeping and organizes it into meaningful financial reports. Accountants also ensure that financial records follow accounting standards and regulations.

While bookkeepers record transactions, accountants focus on interpreting the information and preparing financial statements.

Finance, on the other hand, deals with **managing money and making financial decisions.**

Finance professionals use accounting information to make decisions about investments, funding, budgeting, and business growth.

For example, finance managers might decide:

- whether to expand the business
- how to invest profits
- whether to borrow money
- how to allocate resources

In simple terms:

Bookkeeping records financial activity.
Accounting organizes and reports financial information.
Finance uses that information to make strategic decisions.

These three fields work together. Bookkeeping provides the data, accounting structures the information, and finance uses the insights to guide the future of the business.

Understanding this relationship helps explain why financial accounting plays such a critical role. It serves as the **bridge between raw financial data and informed decision-making**.

Why Businesses Depend on Accounting

No business can operate effectively without reliable financial information. Even the smallest business must track income and expenses to understand whether it is profitable.

Accounting helps businesses answer essential questions such as:

- Are we making money?
- Are our expenses too high?
- Can we afford to hire more employees?
- Should we invest in new equipment?
- Do we have enough cash to continue operating?

Without accounting, business owners would have to rely on guesswork.

Imagine a small bakery that sells cakes, bread, and pastries. Every day, customers buy products and the bakery receives cash. At the same time, the bakery pays for ingredients, electricity, employee wages, and rent.

If the bakery owner does not track these financial activities carefully, it would be impossible to know whether the business is profitable.

It might seem like the bakery is doing well because customers are constantly buying products. But if expenses are higher than revenue, the business could actually be losing money.

Accounting prevents this kind of confusion by providing clear financial records.

Beyond profit tracking, accounting also helps businesses manage their resources effectively.

For example, accounting can reveal:

- which products generate the most profit
- which expenses are increasing
- whether inventory is being managed efficiently
- whether cash flow is stable

This information allows business owners and managers to make smarter decisions.

Accounting is also essential for **building trust.**

Investors, lenders, and partners need accurate financial information before they commit their money to a business.

Banks, for instance, will usually require financial statements before approving a business loan. These statements help the bank evaluate whether the business can repay the loan.

Government agencies also rely on accounting information for tax reporting and regulatory compliance.

Without proper accounting records, businesses may struggle to file accurate tax returns or demonstrate compliance with financial regulations.

In short, accounting serves multiple important functions:

- measuring financial performance
- supporting decision-making
- building trust with investors and lenders
- ensuring compliance with laws and regulations
- guiding long-term business planning

For these reasons, accounting is not just a technical requirement. It is a **core part of running a successful business.**

How Accounting Helps You Make Better Decisions

One of the most valuable aspects of accounting is its ability to support better decision-making.

When financial information is organized clearly, it becomes easier to evaluate different options and choose the best course of action.

Consider a simple example.

Imagine a freelance graphic designer deciding whether to raise prices. Without accounting records, the designer might rely on intuition or guesswork.

But with proper financial records, the designer can analyze important factors such as:

- monthly revenue
- operating expenses
- profit margins
- client payment patterns

This information helps the designer determine whether current pricing is sustainable or whether adjustments are necessary.

Accounting also helps businesses identify trends.

For example, if a company notices that sales increase significantly during certain months, it can prepare by increasing inventory or hiring temporary staff during those periods.

Similarly, if expenses are rising faster than revenue, managers can investigate the cause and take corrective action.

Accounting also plays a critical role in budgeting.

A budget is essentially a financial plan for the future. By analyzing past financial data, businesses can estimate future income and expenses more accurately.

This helps organizations allocate resources more effectively and avoid unexpected financial difficulties.

Accounting information can also guide investment decisions.

Suppose a business is considering purchasing new equipment. Accounting records can reveal whether the company has enough resources to afford the purchase or whether financing might be required.

Even individuals benefit from accounting principles.

For example, a freelancer managing multiple clients might use accounting tools to track income and expenses. This makes it easier to plan taxes, monitor profitability, and make financial decisions about business growth.

In all these situations, accounting transforms financial data into actionable insights.

Instead of relying on assumptions or emotions, decision-makers can rely on clear financial evidence.

This is why accounting is often described as a **decision-support system for businesses**.

It helps people understand not only what has happened financially but also what actions should be taken next.

Real-World Situations Where Accounting Knowledge Matters

Many people assume accounting knowledge is only necessary for accountants. In reality, accounting skills are useful in many everyday situations.

Consider the following real-world examples.

A small business owner wants to open a second location. Before making that decision, the owner needs to evaluate the financial performance of the existing location. Accounting records reveal whether the business generates enough profit to support expansion.

A manager in a retail company receives monthly financial reports. These reports show revenue, expenses, and profit margins. Understanding accounting allows the manager to interpret these numbers and improve store performance.

A startup founder is pitching the business to potential investors. Investors will likely ask questions about revenue growth, operating costs, and profitability.

Accounting knowledge allows the founder to answer these questions confidently.

A freelancer prepares for tax season. Without accurate accounting records, it would be difficult to determine total income, deductible expenses, and taxable profit.

A corporate employee participates in a strategy meeting. Financial reports are presented during the discussion. Employees who understand accounting can contribute more effectively to the conversation.

Even individuals managing personal finances benefit from basic accounting concepts.

For example, understanding the difference between profit and cash flow can help people manage their finances more effectively.

A person might earn a high income but still struggle financially if expenses are not controlled. Accounting principles help clarify these financial relationships.

In modern workplaces, financial awareness is becoming increasingly important. Employees who understand financial reports often gain an advantage because they can connect their work to the financial performance of the organization.

Entrepreneurs also benefit greatly from accounting knowledge.

Many small businesses fail not because the product or service is poor, but because the owners do not understand the financial side of the business.

Without clear financial records, it is difficult to control costs, manage cash flow, or plan for growth.

Accounting provides the tools needed to avoid these challenges.

As you continue through this book, you will learn how financial information is recorded, organized, and interpreted. Each concept builds on the previous one, gradually developing your understanding of how businesses manage financial information.

CHAPTER 2

HOW MONEY FLOWS THROUGH A BUSINESS

Before diving deeper into accounting systems and financial statements, it is important to understand a simple but powerful idea: **every business is essentially a flow of money**. Money comes in, money goes out, and the difference between those movements tells the story of whether the business is thriving or struggling.

Financial accounting exists to track this flow clearly and accurately. Without it, a business owner might see sales happening every day but still have no real understanding of profitability, financial health, or long-term sustainability.

Think of a business like a **living system.** Just as blood circulates through the human body carrying oxygen and nutrients, money circulates through a business carrying the resources needed for operations, growth, and stability. When that flow is healthy and well-managed, the business can survive and expand. When it is poorly tracked or poorly managed, problems can quickly arise.

In this chapter, we will explore how money moves through a business and why understanding this movement is essential. We will look at the core financial elements that every business deals with—revenue, expenses, assets, liabilities, and equity and explain how these elements interact to form the foundation of financial accounting.

By the end of this chapter, you will have a clear understanding of how businesses generate money, how they spend it, how they keep track of it, and why every financial transaction plays a role in shaping the overall financial picture.

UNDERSTANDING REVENUE AND EXPENSES

At the heart of every business are two basic financial forces: **revenue and expenses**.

Revenue represents the money a business earns from providing goods or services to customers. Expenses represent the money the business spends in order to operate and generate that revenue.

Understanding these two concepts is the first step toward understanding how businesses measure success.

Imagine a small coffee shop located in a busy neighborhood. Every day customers come in and purchase coffee, pastries, and sandwiches. The money collected from those sales is the shop's **revenue**.

However, running the coffee shop requires many costs. The owner must purchase coffee beans, milk, pastries, cups, and napkins. Employees must be paid wages. The shop must pay rent, electricity, internet service, and cleaning supplies.

All of these costs are **expenses**.

At the end of the day, week, or month, the owner compares the revenue earned with the expenses incurred. If revenue is greater than expenses, the business has made a **profit**. If expenses exceed revenue, the business experiences a **loss**.

This simple relationship can be summarized like this:

Revenue – Expenses = Profit (or Loss)

While this formula appears simple, it represents one of the most important measurements in business.

A company might appear busy and successful from the outside, but if expenses are constantly higher than revenue, the business cannot survive for long.

Let’s look at a simple example.

Suppose the coffee shop earns $8,000 in revenue during a month. During the same month, it spends:

- $2,000 on ingredients
- $2,500 on employee wages
- $1,500 on rent
- $500 on utilities
- $300 on supplies

Total expenses equal $6,800.

When we subtract expenses from revenue:

$8,000 – $6,800 = $1,200 profit.

This means the coffee shop generated $1,200 in profit for that month.

For many beginners, accounting becomes much easier when they realize that most financial reporting ultimately revolves around **tracking revenue and expenses accurately**.

However, there is another important insight here. Revenue does not automatically mean cash profit. Sometimes businesses make sales but do not receive payment immediately. Likewise, some expenses may not be paid right away.

This is why accounting systems exist—to carefully track these movements so businesses understand the true financial situation.

As businesses grow, revenue and expenses become more complex. A company may have multiple revenue streams, dozens of expense categories, and thousands of transactions each month. But the core principle remains the same: **track income, track costs, and measure the difference.**

ASSETS, LIABILITIES, AND EQUITY IN SIMPLE TERMS

While revenue and expenses describe how money moves through a business during a period of time, another set of concepts describes the **overall financial position of a business at a specific moment.**

These concepts are **assets, liabilities, and equity.**

Understanding these three ideas is crucial because they form the foundation of the accounting equation, which we will explore later in the book.

Let's start with assets.

Assets are **things a business owns that have value.** These resources help the business operate and generate revenue.

Common examples of assets include:

- Cash in the bank
- Equipment and machinery
- Buildings or office space
- Inventory
- Vehicles
- Computers and technology
- Money owed by customers

If something contributes economic value to the business and can be used to support operations, it is typically considered an asset.

Next, we have liabilities.

Liabilities represent **what the business owes to others.** These are financial obligations that must eventually be paid.

Examples of liabilities include:

- Business loans

- Credit card balances
- Unpaid bills
- Salaries owed to employees
- Taxes owed to the government

Liabilities are essentially claims against the company's assets.

Finally, we have equity.

Equity represents **the owner's stake in the business.** It reflects the portion of the business that belongs to the owner after all liabilities have been accounted for.

A helpful way to think about equity is to imagine selling the business today. After paying off all debts and obligations, whatever remains belongs to the owner. That remaining value is equity.

To illustrate these concepts, imagine a small landscaping company.

The company owns:

- $10,000 in equipment
- $5,000 in cash
- $3,000 in vehicles

These resources total $18,000 in assets.

However, the company also owes:

- $6,000 on a vehicle loan
- $2,000 in unpaid supplier invoices

These obligations total $8,000 in liabilities.

The difference between assets and liabilities is the owner's equity.

Assets ($18,000) – Liabilities ($8,000) = Equity ($10,000)

This simple relationship forms the basis of the accounting equation that all accounting systems rely on.

Assets represent resources. Liabilities represent obligations. Equity represents ownership value.

Together, they describe the financial structure of a business.

HOW BUSINESSES TRACK INCOME AND COSTS

Understanding revenue and expenses conceptually is one thing. Tracking them accurately in real life is another.

Businesses generate dozens, hundreds, or even thousands of financial transactions over time. Each purchase, sale, payment, or expense represents a piece of financial information that must be recorded.

Without a system for tracking these transactions, financial confusion would quickly arise.

This is where accounting systems come into play.

Businesses track income and costs through organized financial records. These records typically include invoices, receipts, bank statements, payroll records, and other documentation.

When a customer purchases a product, the sale is recorded as revenue. When the business pays for supplies or services, the cost is recorded as an expense.

Many small businesses use accounting software to simplify this process. These tools automatically categorize transactions, generate reports, and help business owners see their financial performance clearly.

However, even with modern technology, the underlying process remains the same.

Each transaction must be:

1. **Identified**
2. **Recorded**
3. **Classified**
4. **Summarized**

For example, consider a freelance photographer who completes a project for a client and receives $1,000.

That transaction would be recorded as revenue.

Later, the photographer purchases camera equipment for $300 and pays $50 for photo editing software. These purchases would be recorded as expenses.

Over time, these records accumulate and provide a clear picture of the business's financial activity.

At the end of the month or year, the accumulated information is organized into financial reports that summarize income and costs.

Accurate tracking allows business owners to answer critical questions:

- Which services generate the most income?
- Which expenses are increasing?
- Are profits improving over time?
- Are operating costs under control?

Without careful tracking, these insights would remain hidden.

THE FINANCIAL LIFE CYCLE OF A BUSINESS

Every business goes through a repeating cycle of financial activity. Understanding this cycle helps explain why accounting systems exist.

The cycle typically begins with **investment or funding**.

When a business starts, it needs resources. These resources may come from the owner's personal investment, loans from banks, or funding from investors.

Once the business has funding, it can acquire assets such as equipment, inventory, and workspace.

Next comes **operation**.

The business uses its resources to produce goods or services. During this stage, the business generates revenue from customers while also incurring expenses related to operations.

For example, a bakery purchases ingredients, hires staff, and sells baked goods. The revenue from customers supports ongoing operations.

The next stage involves **financial recording and reporting**.

All business transactions are recorded in the accounting system. These records allow the business to prepare financial reports showing income, expenses, assets, and liabilities.

These reports help owners and managers evaluate performance and plan future strategies.

Finally, the cycle leads to **decision-making and growth**.

Based on financial information, the business may decide to expand operations, invest in new equipment, hire additional employees, or adjust pricing strategies.

These decisions generate new financial transactions, and the cycle continues.

This ongoing financial cycle explains why accounting is essential. Without accurate financial records, businesses would struggle to evaluate performance or make informed decisions about the future.

WHY EVERY TRANSACTION MATTERS

One of the most important lessons in accounting is that **every transaction affects the financial story of a business**.

At first, some transactions may seem small or insignificant. A purchase of office supplies, a small payment from a customer, or a utility bill might appear trivial on their own.

However, when hundreds or thousands of transactions accumulate over time, they shape the overall financial picture.

Consider a small online retail business.

Each day the business processes dozens of orders, purchases inventory, pays shipping fees, and manages advertising costs.

If these transactions are not recorded properly, the business owner may struggle to understand whether the company is truly profitable.

Even small recording errors can create confusion. For example, failing to record a recurring expense could make profits appear larger than they really are.

Likewise, forgetting to record customer payments could make revenue appear lower than it actually is.

Accurate transaction tracking ensures that financial reports reflect reality.

Another reason transactions matter is that they affect multiple parts of the financial system simultaneously.

A sale increases revenue.
Receiving payment increases cash.
Purchasing equipment increases assets.
Taking a loan increases liabilities.

Each action changes the financial structure of the business.

This is why accounting systems carefully record every transaction and maintain balance across financial records.

As we move forward in this book, you will learn how these transactions are recorded, organized, and summarized into financial statements.

Understanding how money flows through a business is the first step toward mastering financial accounting.

Once you see how revenue, expenses, assets, liabilities, and transactions interact, accounting begins to feel far less intimidating.

Instead of seeing accounting as complicated mathematics, you begin to see it for what it truly is: **a structured way of telling the financial story of a business.**

CHAPTER 3

THE LANGUAGE OF ACCOUNTING

One reason accounting feels difficult to beginners is not always the numbers. More often, it is the language. The subject comes with its own vocabulary, and when those words are unfamiliar, even a simple explanation can feel harder than it should. A person may read terms like *assets*, *liabilities*, *equity*, *accruals*, *accounts receivable*, or *depreciation* and immediately feel shut out, as though accounting belongs to a private club with its own code words.

But once the language becomes familiar, the subject starts to open up. The fog clears. Financial statements begin to look less like intimidating reports and more like organized stories about what a business owns, what it owes, what it earns, what it spends, and what remains.

That is really what accounting language does. It gives names to the most important parts of a business's financial life. These words are not there to confuse people. They exist because businesses need a clear way to describe money, value, responsibility, performance, and ownership.

Think of accounting language the way you might think of road signs in a new city. At first, the symbols and directions can feel overwhelming. But once you understand what each sign means, moving around becomes easier, safer, and more confident. The same is true here. When you know what the words mean, you can read financial information without feeling lost.

This part of the journey is about becoming fluent in the basic vocabulary of accounting. Not in a dry, dictionary-like way, but in a practical way. The goal is to make the words feel familiar enough that when you see them in a report, hear them in a meeting, or come across them in a business conversation, you immediately understand what they are pointing to.

ESSENTIAL ACCOUNTING TERMS EVERY BEGINNER SHOULD KNOW

Every field has a set of foundational words that carry most of the meaning. In accounting, there are several terms that appear again and again. Once these become second nature, the rest of the subject becomes easier to follow.

Let us begin with one of the broadest terms: **account.**

In everyday language, the word *account* can mean a bank account or even a version of an event, as in "my account of what happened." In accounting, an account is simply a category used to record a certain type of financial activity or financial value. A business may have a cash account, a rent expense account, a sales revenue account, an equipment account, and many others. Each account acts like a labeled container where similar financial information is grouped together.

Then there is **transaction.**

A transaction is any financial event that affects the business and can be recorded. Selling a product, paying rent, buying supplies, receiving a loan, or investing personal money into the business are all transactions. If it changes the company's financial position in some measurable way, it is a transaction.

Another core term is **cash.**

Cash does not only mean physical notes and coins. In accounting, it usually refers to money that is immediately available, including money in a business bank account. Cash is one of the most important resources a company has because it is the most liquid asset, meaning it can be used right away.

That leads naturally to **asset.**

An asset is something valuable that a business owns or controls and can use to operate or generate future benefits. Cash is an asset. Equipment is an asset. Inventory is an asset. A company vehicle is an asset. Money owed to the business by customers is also an asset because the business expects to receive that money.

The term **liability** refers to an obligation. It is something the business owes to someone else. A bank loan is a liability. Unpaid supplier bills are liabilities. Salaries owed to employees are liabilities. Taxes due but not yet paid are liabilities. If an asset represents value the business has, a liability represents value the business must give up in the future.

Equity is the owner's share of the business. It is what remains after subtracting liabilities from assets. If a business owns assets worth $50,000 and owes $20,000, the remaining $30,000 belongs to the owner in the form of equity. This concept is central because it shows how much of the business truly belongs to its owner after all debts are accounted for.

Another word that appears frequently is **revenue**.

Revenue is the income a business earns from its main activities, such as selling goods or providing services. For a bakery, revenue comes from selling bread and cakes. For a freelance designer, revenue comes from client work. For a consulting firm, revenue comes from professional services.

Expense is the cost incurred in order to run the business and earn revenue. Rent, wages, internet bills, software subscriptions, advertising, utilities, raw materials, and office supplies are all examples of expenses.

Profit is what remains after expenses are deducted from revenue. It is a measure of whether the business is financially gaining ground. If revenue exceeds expenses, there is profit. If expenses exceed revenue, there is a loss.

You will also come across **income**. In many contexts, income is used similarly to revenue or profit, depending on the setting. In accounting, the precise meaning depends on the statement or report being used. This is why context matters. Sometimes "income" refers to earnings before expenses are deducted, and sometimes it refers to final profit after costs are considered. Careful reading helps avoid confusion.

Accounts receivable is money customers owe the business for goods or services already provided. Imagine a company that delivers office furniture to a corporate client and gives the client 30 days to pay. The sale has happened, but the cash has not yet arrived. Until payment is received, that amount is recorded as accounts receivable.

Accounts payable is the opposite. It refers to money the business owes to suppliers or vendors for goods or services already received. If a restaurant receives ingredients from a supplier and is given time to pay later, the amount owed is recorded as accounts payable.

Inventory refers to goods a business holds for sale. In a clothing store, inventory includes shirts, trousers, dresses, and jackets waiting to be sold. In a manufacturing business, inventory might include raw materials, partially finished products, and finished goods.

Depreciation is a term that often sounds more complicated than it really is. It refers to the gradual reduction in the value of a long-term asset over time.

A delivery van, for example, does not stay new forever. It experiences wear and tear. Depreciation is the accounting way of spreading the cost of that asset over the period in which it is used.

Cost of goods sold, often shortened to COGS, refers to the direct costs involved in producing or purchasing the goods sold by the business. For a bakery, it includes flour, sugar, butter, and other ingredients directly used to make products sold to customers. For a retail store, it includes the cost of buying the products that are later resold.

Gross profit is revenue minus cost of goods sold. It shows how much money is left after covering the direct cost of producing or purchasing what was sold, before accounting for other operating expenses like rent or salaries.

Net profit is what remains after all expenses have been deducted. This is often the number business owners watch closely because it reflects the overall result after everything is considered.

Then there are the terms **debit** and **credit**. These words often scare beginners because they sound technical and seem to conflict with the way banks use them. In accounting, they are simply labels used in the double-entry system to show increases and decreases in different types of accounts. They are not automatically “good” or “bad,” nor do they always mean money going in or out. Their meaning depends on the type of account involved.

You will also hear about **journal entries**, which are the first formal records of transactions, and the **ledger**, which is where transactions are organized by account. Then there is the **trial balance**, a report used to check that total debits equal total credits before financial statements are prepared.

It may seem like a lot at first, but the more these words appear in real situations, the more natural they become. Accounting vocabulary is easier to learn when it is tied to real business activity instead of memorized in isolation. A bakery buying flour, a freelancer sending an invoice, a shop paying electricity, or a business owner investing startup funds all bring these terms to life.

REVENUE, EXPENSES, AND PROFIT EXPLAINED

Few ideas matter more in business than the relationship between revenue, expenses, and profit.

These three terms sit at the heart of financial performance. They shape how businesses are judged, how managers make decisions, and how owners understand whether their efforts are paying off.

Revenue is often the easiest to notice because it is the money coming in from customers. If a tailoring shop earns money from sewing clothes, that income is revenue. If a tutoring center collects fees from students, that income is revenue. If an online store sells phone accessories, the money from those sales is revenue.

Revenue tells us the business is active. It shows that customers are willing to pay for what the business offers. But revenue alone does not tell the full story.

A business can generate impressive sales and still struggle financially if its costs are too high. This is where expenses come in.

Expenses are the costs of running the business. They include all the resources used up in the process of earning revenue. A food business may spend money on ingredients, packaging, transportation, staff wages, cooking gas, electricity, rent, and advertising. Those are expenses. A photographer may pay for editing software, camera maintenance, transport to client locations, internet access, and marketing. Those too are expenses.

If revenue is the inflow, expenses are the outflow.

Profit is what remains after those expenses are taken away from revenue. It answers a simple question: after all the effort, cost, and activity, what did the business actually keep?

Imagine a small event planning business that earns $12,000 in a month from client bookings. That sounds encouraging. But during the same month, it spends $3,000 on venue deposits, $2,500 on decorations, $2,000 on staff, $1,000 on transportation, $1,200 on marketing, and $800 on office-related expenses. Total expenses come to $10,500. The profit is $1,500.

Without considering expenses, the owner might focus only on the $12,000 in sales and feel overly confident. But once expenses are included, the real picture becomes clearer.

This is why profit matters so much. It is not just about being busy. It is about whether the business activity is creating enough surplus to justify the effort and sustain the operation.

There are several layers to profit. One common layer is **gross profit**, which measures the difference between revenue and the direct costs of the goods sold. Another is **operating profit**, which takes into account additional operating costs. Finally, **net profit** reflects the amount left after all expenses, including taxes and other costs, have been deducted.

For beginners, the key idea is to avoid assuming that revenue equals success. Strong sales are good, but strong sales combined with controlled costs are much better.

It is also important to understand the difference between profit and cash. A business may record profit on paper but still experience cash pressure. For example, if many customers have not yet paid their invoices, revenue may be recognized, but the business may still have little cash available in the bank. This is one reason accounting looks beyond simple inflows and outflows and tracks timing carefully.

In daily conversation, people often say things like, "The business made a lot of money this month." In accounting, it helps to ask a follow-up question: do they mean revenue, cash received, or actual profit? Those are not always the same thing.

A clothing retailer may sell many items on credit to customers, creating revenue. But if payment has not yet been collected, cash has not increased by the same amount. Likewise, a business may pay expenses for future periods, such as annual insurance, meaning cash leaves the bank now even though the expense may be recognized over time.

This is why precise accounting language matters. It helps separate concepts that are often mixed together in casual speech.

When business owners understand revenue, expenses, and profit clearly, they become better decision-makers. They can price products more intelligently, spot unhealthy spending patterns, and focus on what actually improves financial results rather than what only looks impressive at first glance.

CAPITAL, INVESTMENTS, AND OWNER'S EQUITY

When people start a business, one of the first financial questions is simple and practical: where will the money come from? A business needs resources to begin operating. It may need equipment, stock, tools, furniture, a website, software, rent money, or initial marketing. Those resources do not appear by magic. Someone must provide the funds.

This introduces the ideas of capital, investments, and owner's equity.

Capital is money or other resources put into a business to help it start or operate. In small businesses, this often comes directly from the owner. A person opening a small printing shop may contribute personal savings to buy printers, pay rent, and purchase supplies. That contribution is capital.

Capital can also come in forms other than cash. If the owner contributes a laptop, a vehicle, or equipment for business use, those contributions are also treated as part of capital because they add value to the business.

The word **investment** is closely related but slightly broader. In one sense, when an owner puts personal money into a business, that is an investment. In another sense, outside investors may provide money to the business in exchange for ownership or a future return. An investor may believe the business has strong growth potential and decide to contribute funds to help it expand.

For beginners, it helps to think of capital as the starting fuel and investment as the act of putting that fuel into the business with the expectation that it will produce value.

Now let us talk about **owner's equity**.

Owner's equity represents the owner's financial interest in the business. It reflects what belongs to the owner after business obligations are taken into account. If the business sold all its assets and paid all its debts, whatever remained would belong to the owner. That remaining amount is equity.

At the start of a business, owner's equity is often closely linked to capital contributions. If the owner invests $15,000 to launch the business, the business's equity begins with that amount. Over time, however, equity changes. If the business earns profit and keeps that profit in the business, equity increases. If the owner withdraws money for personal use, equity decreases. If the business suffers losses, equity can also decrease.

A simple example makes this easier to see.

Imagine Rita starts a home bakery. She invests $8,000 of her own money to buy an oven, baking tools, ingredients, and packaging supplies. That initial contribution becomes part of the business's capital and creates owner's equity.

A few months later, the bakery earns a profit of $2,000. Rita leaves that money in the business rather than taking it out for personal use. Her equity increases because the business has grown in value.

Later, she withdraws $500 to pay a personal bill. That withdrawal reduces her equity because she has taken some value out of the business.

This is one reason it is important to separate business finances from personal finances. When owners mix the two carelessly, the true financial picture becomes harder to track.

Another common source of confusion is the difference between **equity** and **liabilities**. Both represent sources of funding, but they are not the same. Equity reflects the owner's claim on the business. Liabilities reflect outsiders' claims. A bank loan gives the bank a claim on the business's resources until the loan is repaid. Owner's equity reflects what belongs to the owner after those outside claims are settled.

In larger businesses, especially companies with multiple investors, equity may be divided into shares. But the basic idea remains the same: equity is the ownership value in the business.

The term **drawings** or **owner's withdrawals** is also worth knowing. This refers to money or assets the owner takes out of the business for personal use. These withdrawals are not expenses of the business. They do not represent the cost of earning revenue. Instead, they are reductions in owner's equity.

This distinction matters. If a business owner treats personal withdrawals as business expenses, the financial statements become misleading. Expenses are costs related to running the business. Owner's withdrawals are distributions of value from the business to the owner.

Once capital, investments, and owner's equity are understood, business financing starts to make more sense. You can begin to see the difference between money the owner has put in, money the business has earned, money the owner has taken out, and money the business owes to others.

UNDERSTANDING FINANCIAL TRANSACTIONS

If accounting is a language, transactions are the sentences that make the language come alive. Every time something financially meaningful happens in a business, a transaction occurs. These transactions are the raw material of accounting. They are what accountants record, classify, summarize, and eventually present in financial statements.

A financial transaction is any event that changes the financial position of a business and can be measured in monetary terms.

That definition may sound formal, but the idea is straightforward. When a business buys inventory, sells a product, pays rent, receives a loan, or purchases equipment, each of those actions changes something financially. The business either gains a resource, gives up a resource, takes on an obligation, earns income, or incurs a cost.

For something to count as an accounting transaction, it usually needs to meet two conditions. First, it must involve the business. Second, it must be measurable in money.

Let us take a few everyday examples.

A freelance writer completes a project and sends an invoice to the client for $600. That is a transaction because the business has earned revenue.

A small supermarket pays $1,200 in rent. That is a transaction because cash decreases and rent expense increases.

A startup founder contributes a laptop worth $900 to the business. That is a transaction because business assets increase and owner's equity increases.

A boutique buys clothing stock from a supplier on credit. That is a transaction because inventory increases and a liability is created.

Now consider a different example. Suppose the owner of a small café has a great idea for adding smoothies to the menu. That idea may be important, but until money is committed or some measurable financial event occurs, it is not yet an accounting transaction. Accounting records actions, not hopes or intentions.

Transactions can be grouped into broad categories.

Some involve **income**, such as sales and service fees earned.

Some involve **expenses**, such as utility bills, wages, and advertising costs.

Some involve **assets**, such as buying equipment or collecting cash from customers.

Some involve **liabilities**, such as taking a loan or receiving goods on credit.

Some involve **equity**, such as owner investments and withdrawals.

What makes accounting powerful is that every transaction affects at least two parts of the financial picture. If a business buys equipment with cash, equipment increases while cash decreases. If a company makes a sale on credit, revenue increases and accounts receivable increases. If wages are paid, cash decreases and wage expense increases.

This is the logic behind the double-entry system, which will become more important later. For now, what matters is understanding that transactions do not float around as isolated events. Each one has an effect, and that effect must be recorded completely.

It helps to think of transactions as footprints. They show where the business has been financially. A single transaction may look small on its own, but over days, weeks, and months, those footprints reveal patterns. They show whether the business is growing, struggling, borrowing too much, spending carelessly, or becoming more profitable.

Financial transactions also depend on timing. Not every business event is recorded only when cash changes hands. If a service is provided today and payment will come next month, accounting still needs to capture that event because value has already been created. Likewise, if a business receives a utility bill today but will pay it later, the obligation already exists and needs to be recognized.

This timing issue is one reason accounting can feel more detailed than simple cash tracking. But that detail is what makes financial information useful. It helps businesses see not only what cash moved, but what was earned, owed, owned, or consumed during a period.

For beginners, one of the best habits is to ask a simple question whenever something happens in a business: what changed financially? Did cash increase? Did a liability arise? Did the business earn revenue? Did an expense occur? That question builds the mindset needed to understand accounting clearly.

COMMON ACCOUNTING TERMS USED IN BUSINESS REPORTS

Once basic accounting language is familiar, the next step is recognizing the terms that often appear in financial reports, business updates, and management discussions. These are the words business owners, managers, accountants, lenders, and investors use when they want to understand how an organization is performing.

One of the most common terms is **sales.** In many businesses, sales refers to revenue earned from selling products or services. In casual business speech, sales and revenue are often used interchangeably, though in formal reporting revenue may be the broader term.

Another frequent term is **gross margin** or **gross profit margin.** This measures how much of each sales dollar remains after direct production or purchase costs are deducted. It helps businesses understand how efficiently they are producing or sourcing what they sell. A strong gross margin often gives a business more room to cover operating costs and still earn profit.

Then there is **operating expense.** These are the regular costs of running the business aside from direct product costs. Rent, salaries, insurance, office supplies, internet service, and marketing often fall into this category. Operating expenses matter because even a business with good sales and strong gross profit can still struggle if everyday running costs are too high.

Net income is another major term. This refers to the final profit after all expenses have been deducted from revenue. In many reports, net income is one of the most closely watched figures because it reflects the overall financial result for the period.

You may also see **current assets** and **current liabilities**. Current assets are assets expected to be used, sold, or converted into cash within a relatively short period, usually one year. Cash, inventory, and accounts receivable are common examples. Current liabilities are obligations expected to be paid within a year, such as supplier invoices, short-term loans, or taxes payable.

These terms matter because they relate to **liquidity**, which is the ability of a business to meet short-term obligations. A profitable business can still face trouble if it does not have enough liquid resources to pay near-term bills.

The term **working capital** builds on this idea. Working capital is generally the difference between current assets and current liabilities. It gives a quick sense of whether a business has enough short-term financial strength to operate comfortably.

Retained earnings is another important phrase. This refers to accumulated profits that have been kept in the business rather than distributed to owners or shareholders. Over time, retained earnings can become a significant part of equity, especially in established businesses that reinvest profits.

Accrued expenses are expenses that have been incurred but not yet paid. For example, employees may have worked during the last week of the month, but wages may not be paid until the next month. The cost belongs to the earlier period because the work has already been done.

Unearned revenue or **deferred revenue** refers to money received before the business has delivered the related goods or services. If a client pays in advance for a training program that will be delivered next month, the business has cash, but it has not yet earned that revenue. Until the service is provided, the amount is treated as a liability.

Prepaid expenses are payments made in advance for future benefits. Insurance premiums paid ahead of time are a common example. Although cash has already left the business, the full amount is not immediately treated as an expense if the benefit extends into future periods.

You will also see **amortization**, which is similar in idea to depreciation but usually applies to intangible assets, and **bad debt**, which refers to money owed by customers that may never be collected.

In management conversations, people often use the phrase **bottom line**. This usually refers to net profit or net income. It comes from the traditional placement of final profit figures at the bottom of the income statement.

Another useful term is **top line**, which refers to revenue. When someone says a company is growing its top line, they mean it is increasing sales or revenue. When they talk about improving the bottom line, they mean it is increasing profit.

The term **cash burn** is common in startups and fast-growing businesses. It refers to the rate at which a business is spending cash, especially when expenses exceed incoming cash. This matters a great deal for young businesses that are not yet consistently profitable.

Break-even point is the level at which total revenue equals total expenses. At that point, the business is not making a profit, but it is not making a loss either. Knowing the break-even point helps owners understand how much they need to sell before the business truly starts earning.

You may also encounter **return on investment**, often called ROI. This measures how much benefit or profit is generated compared with the amount invested. It is a useful way to judge whether spending on equipment, advertising, or expansion was worthwhile.

The reason these terms matter is not simply to sound knowledgeable in a meeting. They shape how businesses are understood and managed. A report may show strong revenue growth, but if working capital is weak and cash burn is high, the business may still be under pressure. Another report may show modest sales, but strong margins and good retained earnings, suggesting healthier long-term performance than first impressions would suggest.

When beginners become comfortable with these terms, financial reports stop feeling like walls of unfamiliar language. They start becoming readable. A person can look at a report and understand what is improving, what is under strain, and what questions need to be asked next.

That is one of the real turning points in learning accounting. The words stop being obstacles and start becoming tools. Instead of staring at business reports and feeling disconnected, you begin to follow the financial conversation with confidence. You understand what is being measured, why it matters, and how the different pieces fit together.

And once that happens, accounting begins to feel less like a difficult subject and more like a practical way of seeing clearly.

CHAPTER 4

THE ACCOUNTING EQUATION

Behind every financial report, ledger entry, and accounting record lies one powerful idea that keeps everything organized. This idea is called the **accounting equation**. It acts like the structural frame of a building. Without it, financial information would collapse into confusion. With it, everything fits together logically.

Businesses deal with thousands of transactions—sales, purchases, payments, investments, loans, and expenses. If these activities were simply written down without a guiding structure, it would be nearly impossible to maintain accurate records. The accounting equation provides that structure.

At its core, the accounting equation explains the relationship between what a business **owns**, what it **owes**, and what **belongs to the owner**. These three elements—assets, liabilities, and equity—work together to describe the financial position of a business at any given moment.

Understanding this relationship is one of the most important steps in learning financial accounting. Once the equation becomes familiar, many other accounting concepts begin to make sense naturally. Journal entries, financial statements, and transaction recording all rely on the same underlying logic.

Instead of memorizing rules without context, the accounting equation gives you a simple mental model for how business finances are organized. Every transaction a business makes must fit into this model. If it does not, something is wrong.

Think of the accounting equation as the **financial balance system** that keeps every business record consistent and reliable.

THE FOUNDATION OF FINANCIAL ACCOUNTING

Imagine trying to keep track of a business's financial situation without any structure. Sales would be recorded somewhere, expenses somewhere else, assets in another place, and debts somewhere entirely different. Over time, the information would become messy and difficult to understand.

Financial accounting avoids this problem by organizing everything around a central principle. That principle is the accounting equation.

This equation provides the framework that holds all financial records together. It ensures that every transaction has a logical place and that financial statements remain accurate.

To understand why this matters, consider how businesses operate. Every organization has resources—things it uses to run the business. These resources might include cash, equipment, inventory, or property.

At the same time, businesses often owe money to others. They may owe suppliers for goods, banks for loans, employees for wages, or governments for taxes.

Finally, whatever remains after these obligations belong to the owner or owners of the business.

Accounting captures this relationship using a simple equation that forms the backbone of the entire system.

Without this equation, accountants would have no consistent way to track how resources are funded or how financial activity affects ownership.

The equation also provides an important safeguard. Because every transaction must keep the equation balanced, it becomes easier to detect mistakes. If the numbers stop balancing, it signals that something has been recorded incorrectly.

In this way, the accounting equation acts like a built-in error detection system. It helps maintain accuracy across financial records.

Another reason this equation is so powerful is that it connects directly to financial statements. The balance sheet, one of the most important financial reports, is essentially a detailed presentation of the accounting equation.

The balance sheet lists assets on one side and liabilities and equity on the other, reflecting the same relationship expressed by the equation.

For beginners, recognizing this connection makes accounting feel less mysterious. Instead of seeing financial reports as complicated documents, they can be viewed as structured reflections of a single underlying idea.

Once the accounting equation becomes familiar, you begin to see it everywhere in business finance.

UNDERSTANDING ASSETS = LIABILITIES + EQUITY

The accounting equation is written as:

Assets = Liabilities + Equity

Although this expression looks simple, it captures the entire financial structure of a business.

Let us break it down piece by piece.

Assets

Assets represent everything the business owns or controls that has value. These resources help the business operate and generate income.

Common assets include:

- Cash
- Inventory
- Equipment
- Vehicles
- Buildings
- Computers
- Money owed by customers (accounts receivable)

Assets can be thought of as the **tools and resources** a business uses to function.

For example, imagine a small bicycle repair shop. The business might own repair tools, spare parts, workbenches, and a small amount of cash in the bank. These are all assets because they contribute to the operation of the business.

Liabilities

Liabilities represent obligations. They are amounts the business owes to other parties.

Common liabilities include:

- Bank loans
- Credit card balances
- Supplier invoices
- Taxes payable
- Employee wages owed

If assets represent resources, liabilities represent **claims against those resources**.

For instance, if the bicycle shop took a loan to buy repair equipment, that loan becomes a liability. The shop now has an obligation to repay the bank.

Equity

Equity represents the owner's claim on the business after liabilities have been considered.

It reflects the value that belongs to the owner.

Equity can come from several sources:

- The owner's initial investment
- Additional investments made later
- Profits retained in the business
- Losses that reduce ownership value

Continuing with the bicycle repair shop example, suppose the owner invested personal savings to start the business. That investment becomes part of the owner's equity.

If the business earns profit over time and the owner leaves those profits in the company, equity increases.

Now we can see how the equation fits together.

The assets of a business must always come from somewhere. They are either financed by borrowing money (liabilities) or by the owner's investment and retained profits (equity).

This is why the equation is written as:

Assets = Liabilities + Equity

It simply states that the resources of a business are funded by two sources: creditors and owners.

Understanding this relationship is key to interpreting financial reports and understanding how businesses are financed.

HOW TRANSACTIONS AFFECT THE ACCOUNTING EQUATION

Every financial transaction a business makes affects the accounting equation in some way.

However, the most important rule is this:

The equation must always remain balanced.

Whenever a transaction occurs, at least two parts of the equation change, but the balance is preserved.

Let us explore several common scenarios.

Owner Investment

Suppose an entrepreneur starts a small photography business and invests $5,000 of personal savings into the business bank account.

The business now has $5,000 in cash, which is an asset.

At the same time, the owner's equity increases by $5,000 because the owner has invested that money.

The equation now looks like this:

Assets: $5,000
Liabilities: $0
Equity: $5,000

The equation remains balanced.

Buying Equipment with Cash

Next, imagine the photographer purchases camera equipment for $2,000 using business cash.

One asset (cash) decreases by $2,000. Another asset (equipment) increases by $2,000.

The total value of assets remains the same, and liabilities and equity are unchanged.

The equation stays balanced.

Taking a Loan

Suppose the business takes a $3,000 loan from the bank.

Cash increases by $3,000, which increases assets.

At the same time, the business now owes the bank $3,000, creating a liability.

Assets increase by $3,000, and liabilities increase by $3,000.

Again, the equation remains balanced.

Earning Revenue

Now imagine the photographer completes a project and receives $800 from a client.

Cash increases by $800.

At the same time, the business has earned revenue, which increases equity.

Assets increase by $800 and equity increases by $800.

The equation stays balanced.

Paying Expenses

Suppose the photographer spends $200 on advertising.

Cash decreases by $200.

At the same time, equity decreases because expenses reduce the owner's claim on the business.

Assets decrease by $200 and equity decreases by $200.

Once again, balance is preserved.

These examples illustrate an important idea: every transaction affects the equation in a logical way.

Assets may increase or decrease.
Liabilities may increase or decrease.
Equity may increase or decrease.

But the relationship between the two sides of the equation must always hold true.

SIMPLE EXAMPLES OF THE ACCOUNTING EQUATION IN ACTION

Seeing the accounting equation in real-world situations helps make it easier to understand.

Let us walk through a simple example involving a small bakery.

Step 1: Owner Investment

Maria opens a bakery and invests $10,000 of her own money.

Assets (cash) = $10,000
Liabilities = $0
Equity = $10,000

Step 2: Buy Baking Equipment

Maria buys ovens and baking tools for $4,000.

Cash decreases by $4,000.
Equipment increases by $4,000.

Total assets remain $10,000.

Assets = $10,000
Liabilities = $0
Equity = $10,000

Step 3: Purchase Ingredients on Credit

Maria buys flour, sugar, and other supplies for $1,500 from a supplier, agreeing to pay later.

Inventory increases by $1,500.
Liabilities increase by $1,500.

Assets = $11,500
Liabilities = $1,500
Equity = $10,000

Step 4: Sell Baked Goods

During the first week, Maria sells baked goods for $2,000 in cash.

Cash increases by $2,000.
Revenue increases equity by $2,000.

Assets = $13,500
Liabilities = $1,500
Equity = $12,000

Step 5: Pay Supplier

Maria pays the supplier $1,500.

Cash decreases by $1,500.
Liabilities decrease by $1,500.

Assets = $12,000
Liabilities = $0
Equity = $12,000

Throughout every step, the accounting equation remained balanced.

This example shows how the equation captures the financial story of a business as it grows and operates.

WHY THE ACCOUNTING EQUATION ALWAYS BALANCES

One of the most powerful features of the accounting equation is that it **must always balance**.

This is not just a theoretical idea. It is a direct result of how financial transactions work.

Every asset owned by a business must be financed by either borrowing money or by the owner's investment.

Because of this, any change in assets must be matched by a change in liabilities or equity.

For example:

If a business buys equipment with cash, one asset replaces another.

If a business borrows money, assets increase and liabilities increase.

If a business earns profit, assets increase and equity increases.

If a business pays expenses, assets decrease and equity decreases.

The relationship between the two sides of the equation remains intact.

This balancing principle is the reason accounting systems use **double-entry recording**, which ensures that every transaction affects at least two accounts.

It also explains why accountants use trial balances and financial statements to verify accuracy. If the numbers stop balancing, it signals that an error has occurred.

Beyond its role in recordkeeping, the accounting equation also provides a deeper insight into how businesses operate.

It shows that every business resource must be financed by someone. Either creditors provide funding through loans and obligations, or owners provide funding through investments and retained profits.

Once you understand this relationship, financial statements begin to make much more sense. The numbers stop feeling random and start telling a logical story.

The accounting equation is not just a formula. It is the organizing principle that supports the entire structure of financial accounting.

Every balance sheet reflects it.
Every transaction respects it.
Every financial record depends on it.

When this idea becomes clear, the rest of accounting starts to fall into place naturally.

CHAPTER 5

THE DOUBLE-ENTRY ACCOUNTING SYSTEM

There is a moment in learning accounting when everything starts to feel more technical. For many beginners, that moment arrives with two words: **debits** and **credits**. People hear them and immediately assume accounting is about memorizing strange rules or doing mental gymnastics every time money moves. But the truth is far less intimidating.

The double-entry system exists for a simple reason: businesses need a reliable way to record the full effect of every financial event. Money does not move in isolation. If cash comes in, something else changes too. If equipment is purchased, one resource increases while another decreases, or perhaps a debt is created. Every transaction has two sides, and the accounting system is built to capture both.

That is what makes double-entry accounting so powerful. It does not just list activity. It shows the relationship between causes and effects inside the business. It keeps records complete. It keeps reports balanced. Most of all, it helps a business tell the truth about what happened financially.

A good way to think about it is to imagine a seesaw. If one side moves, the other side must respond. Or picture a before-and-after photo. A transaction changes the financial picture, and accounting needs to show exactly what changed and where. The double-entry system is the method that makes that possible.

Once the logic clicks, debits and credits stop looking like abstract accounting code. They become labels for change. They show how transactions reshape the business bit by bit, one entry at a time.

WHY ACCOUNTING USES TWO ENTRIES FOR EVERY TRANSACTION

Every business transaction affects at least two parts of the financial picture. That is not an accounting preference. It is simply how business reality works.

Suppose a business owner buys a laptop for the company using cash. The business now has a new asset, the laptop. At the same time, it has less cash. One thing came in, another went out. If the records only showed the laptop being added but failed to show the cash leaving, the books would be misleading. They would make the business look richer than it really is.

Now imagine the owner borrows money from a bank. Cash increases, which is good for the business, but the business also takes on a liability. If the record only showed the extra cash and ignored the loan, it would paint a dangerously incomplete picture.

This is why accounting uses two entries for every transaction. It is designed to record the full event, not just the most obvious part of it.

The double-entry system rests on the accounting equation:

Assets = Liabilities + Equity

Every transaction must fit within that structure. If one side changes, the other side must change in a way that keeps the equation balanced. That balance is not just a neat idea. It is the reason financial statements can be trusted.

Take a simple service business. A freelance editor completes a project and receives $500 from a client. The business now has $500 more in cash, which means assets increased. But that money did not appear out of nowhere. It was earned through business activity, so equity increases too, because income increases the owner's claim on the business.

Or suppose the editor pays $60 for internet service. Cash decreases, which lowers assets. At the same time, the business records an expense, and that expense reduces equity because it lowers profit.

In both cases, two entries are needed because two parts of the financial story changed.

This system gives accounting a built-in discipline. It forces the person recording transactions to ask, "What came in? What went out? What increased? What decreased? What is the matching effect?" That habit reduces sloppiness and makes the records far more reliable than a one-sided system ever could.

It also helps catch errors. If entries do not balance, something has likely been missed or recorded incorrectly. That is one reason the double-entry system has survived for centuries. It is practical, structured, and surprisingly elegant once you understand the reasoning behind it.

At first, beginners sometimes wish accounting were simpler, more like a basic list of money received and money spent. But that kind of simplicity would fail the moment the business did anything beyond the most basic cash transactions. Credit sales, unpaid bills, owner investments, equipment purchases, and business loans would all become difficult to track accurately. Double-entry accounting solves that problem by treating every transaction as a complete event, not a partial snapshot.

UNDERSTANDING DEBITS AND CREDITS

Debits and credits are often where people tense up. The words sound formal, and to make matters worse, they do not always match the way people use similar terms in everyday banking. A bank statement might show a credit as money added to your account and a debit as money taken out. Accounting uses the same words in a broader and more structured way, which is where confusion often begins.

In accounting, **debit** and **credit** are not moral judgments, and they are not automatically "good" or "bad." They are simply labels used to record how accounts change.

That is the key idea: debits and credits are recording directions.

A debit is entered on the left side of an account. A credit is entered on the right side of an account.

That sounds almost too simple, but it is the foundation. Their meaning depends on the type of account involved.

This is where many beginners trip. They try to memorize "debit means increase" or "credit means decrease." That approach quickly falls apart because debits increase some accounts and decrease others. Credits do the same.

A much better way to understand them is to group accounts into two broad families.

One family includes:

- Assets
- Expenses
- Drawings or owner withdrawals

The other family includes:

- Liabilities
- Equity
- Revenue

For the first family, **debits increase** and **credits decrease.**

For the second family, **credits increase** and **debits decrease.**

That is the pattern.

So if cash increases, cash is an asset, and assets increase with debits.
If rent expense increases, expenses increase with debits.
If a loan increases, liabilities increase with credits.
If sales revenue increases, revenue increases with credits.

It helps to pause here and let that settle because this is one of the most important patterns in beginner accounting.

Here is another way to think about it. The left side of the accounting equation is assets. The right side is liabilities and equity. Debits naturally support the left side, while credits naturally support the right side. Expenses and withdrawals reduce equity, but in the recording system they behave like the debit side, while revenue supports equity and behaves like the credit side.

If that feels a little abstract, the examples will make it more concrete.

Suppose a business receives cash from a customer for a completed service:

- Cash increases, so cash is **debited**
- Revenue increases, so service revenue is **credited**

Suppose a business pays electricity:

- Electricity expense increases, so expense is **debited**
- Cash decreases, so cash is **credited**

Suppose the owner invests money into the business:

- Cash increases, so cash is **debited**
- Owner's capital or owner's equity increases, so equity is **credited**

The logic stays consistent. One entry goes on the left, the other on the right, and total debits must always equal total credits.

A useful mental shift is to stop asking, "Is debit good or bad?" and start asking, "What type of account is this, and which side makes it go up or down?"

That question is much more helpful.

Another common source of confusion is the word **credit** itself. In everyday conversation, credit often means borrowing ability, like when someone says they have good credit. In accounting, a credit is just the right-hand entry. It may increase a liability account, but it does not always mean debt. Revenue accounts increase with credits, and revenue is not debt. Equity increases with credits, and equity is not debt either.

Likewise, a debit does not automatically mean expense or loss. Asset accounts increase with debits, and assets are valuable resources. So it is important not to attach emotional meaning to either term.

Debits and credits are best understood as neutral tools. They help maintain order inside the system. Once that neutral mindset settles in, a lot of the fear disappears.

HOW ACCOUNTS INCREASE AND DECREASE

Now that the idea of debits and credits is on the table, the next step is to see how different accounts behave. This is where the double-entry system begins to feel more practical.

Every account has a normal side, meaning the side that increases it.

For asset accounts, the normal balance is a **debit.** For expense accounts, the normal balance is a **debit.** For withdrawal accounts, the normal balance is a **debit.**

For liability accounts, the normal balance is a **credit.** For equity accounts, the normal balance is a **credit.** For revenue accounts, the normal balance is a **credit.**

When you know the normal side of an account, increases and decreases become easier to understand.

Let us walk through the main account types one by one.

Assets

Assets are resources the business owns or controls. Cash, inventory, equipment, vehicles, and accounts receivable all fall into this category.

Assets increase with debits and decrease with credits.

If a business receives cash from a customer, cash goes up, so cash is debited.

If a business spends cash on rent, cash goes down, so cash is credited.

Liabilities

Liabilities are obligations the business owes to others. Loans, accounts payable, wages payable, and taxes payable are examples.

Liabilities increase with credits and decrease with debits.

If a business takes a bank loan, the liability increases, so loan payable is credited. If the business repays part of that loan, the liability decreases, so loan payable is debited.

Equity

Equity represents the owner's claim on the business. It grows when the owner invests more money or when the business earns profits and keeps them. It shrinks through losses or owner withdrawals.

Equity increases with credits and decreases with debits.

If the owner contributes money to the business, owner's equity is credited.

If the owner withdraws money for personal use, drawings or withdrawals are debited, which reduces equity overall.

Revenue

Revenue is what the business earns from selling goods or providing services.

Revenue increases with credits and decreases with debits.

If a consultant earns a service fee, service revenue is credited.

If a sales return must be recorded in a simplified setting, the adjustment can involve reducing revenue through a debit.

Expenses

Expenses are the costs of operating the business, such as rent, wages, advertising, utilities, and supplies used up.

Expenses increase with debits and decrease with credits.

If a business pays rent, rent expense is debited. If an expense entry must be reversed or corrected, the expense account may be credited.

This pattern may feel like a lot, but it becomes manageable when you realize that most beginner transactions follow a few common routes. Cash comes in and is debited. Cash goes out and is credited. Revenue earned is credited. Expenses incurred are debited. Loans taken are credited as liabilities. Owner investment is credited as equity.

A helpful shortcut many learners use is this:

DEALER

- Dividends or Drawings
- Expenses
- Assets

These increase with **debits**

- Liabilities
- Equity
- Revenue

These increase with **credits**

Even if you do not rely on a memory aid long-term, it can help in the early stages.

The deeper point is this: account movement is not random. Every account follows a pattern, and once you understand that pattern, recording transactions becomes much less intimidating. You stop guessing. You begin identifying.

When a transaction happens, ask:

1. Which accounts are involved?
2. Are they increasing or decreasing?
3. What side records that change?

That three-step thinking is far more effective than trying to force the rules into memory without context.

EXAMPLES OF DOUBLE-ENTRY TRANSACTIONS

Nothing brings accounting to life like real examples. The logic becomes much clearer when you can see how actual business events are recorded.

Let us use a small business called **Bright Start Printing**, a neighborhood print shop that designs flyers, prints brochures, and produces business cards.

Example 1: Owner invests cash into the business

The owner starts the business by putting in $10,000.

What changes?

- Cash increases
- Owner's equity increases

How is it recorded?

- Debit Cash $10,000
- Credit Owner's Capital $10,000

Why? Cash is an asset, and assets increase with debits. Owner's capital is equity, and equity increases with credits.

Example 2: Buy equipment with cash

The business buys printing equipment for $3,000 cash.

What changes?

- Equipment increases
- Cash decreases

How is it recorded?

- Debit Equipment $3,000

- Credit Cash $3,000

Why? Equipment is an asset increasing, so debit it. Cash is an asset decreasing, so credit it.

This example is helpful because it shows that not all transactions affect revenue or expenses. Sometimes one asset simply changes form into another.

Example 3: Purchase paper supplies on credit

The shop buys paper and ink worth $1,200 from a supplier and will pay later.

What changes?

- Supplies or inventory increase
- Accounts payable increases

How is it recorded?

- Debit Supplies $1,200
- Credit Accounts Payable $1,200

Why? Supplies are an asset increasing, so debit. Accounts payable is a liability increasing, so credit.

Example 4: Earn revenue in cash

The shop completes a rush print job and receives $800 cash.

What changes?

- Cash increases
- Revenue increases

How is it recorded?

- Debit Cash $800
- Credit Service Revenue $800

Why? Cash as an asset increases with a debit. Revenue increases with a credit.

Example 5: Earn revenue on credit

A corporate client orders branded materials worth $1,500 and will pay next month.

What changes?

- Accounts receivable increases
- Revenue increases

How is it recorded?

- Debit Accounts Receivable $1,500
- Credit Service Revenue $1,500

Why? Accounts receivable is an asset because the business has a right to collect money. It increases with a debit. Revenue increases with a credit.

This example matters because it shows that money does not need to be received immediately for revenue to be recorded in many accounting situations.

Example 6: Pay rent

The business pays monthly rent of $600.

What changes?

- Rent expense increases
- Cash decreases

How is it recorded?

- Debit Rent Expense $600
- Credit Cash $600

Why? Expenses increase with debits. Cash decreases with credits.

Example 7: Pay part of an amount owed to a supplier

The business pays $500 toward the paper supplies purchased earlier on credit.

What changes?

- Accounts payable decreases
- Cash decreases

How is it recorded?

- Debit Accounts Payable $500
- Credit Cash $500

Why? Accounts payable is a liability. Since the business now owes less, the liability decreases, and liabilities decrease with debits. Cash decreases with credits.

Example 8: Owner withdraws money for personal use

The owner takes $300 from the business bank account for a personal emergency.

What changes?

- Drawings increase
- Cash decreases

How is it recorded?

- Debit Owner's Drawings $300
- Credit Cash $300

Why? Drawings reduce owner's equity and behave like a debit account. Cash decreases with a credit.

This is a useful reminder that personal withdrawals are not business expenses. They should not be recorded as rent expense, salary expense, or miscellaneous expense. They are withdrawals by the owner.

Example 9: Repay part of a bank loan

The business repays $1,000 of a bank loan.

What changes?

- Loan payable decreases
- Cash decreases

How is it recorded?

- Debit Loan Payable $1,000
- Credit Cash $1,000

Why? Loan payable is a liability. Since the business owes less, the account is debited. Cash decreases, so cash is credited.

Example 10: Pay for advertising

The business runs a local social media promotion and pays $250.

What changes?

- Advertising expense increases
- Cash decreases

How is it recorded?

- Debit Advertising Expense $250
- Credit Cash $250

Why? Expense accounts increase with debits. Cash decreases with credits.

What you may notice across all these examples is that the logic is consistent. There is always a give-and-take. Something rises, something falls, or two categories rise together from different sides of the equation.

With enough examples, the double-entry system starts to feel less like a set of rules and more like a structured way of describing reality.

COMMON BEGINNER MISTAKES WITH DEBITS AND CREDITS

Most beginners do not struggle because they are incapable of learning accounting. They struggle because the early mistakes are so common that they can make the whole system feel harder than it really is. Once those traps are identified, the path becomes much smoother.

One very common mistake is assuming that **debit always means increase** and **credit always means decrease**.

That seems logical at first, but it is not true across all accounts. Debits increase assets and expenses, but they decrease liabilities, equity, and revenue. Credits do the reverse. The fix is simple: always identify the type of account before deciding how to record the change.

Another common mistake is confusing accounting language with banking language. On a personal bank statement, a credit may mean money added to your account, which leads many people to assume cash should always be credited when it increases. In accounting, cash is an asset, and assets increase with debits. This mismatch causes a lot of early frustration.

The best way around it is to treat accounting as its own system rather than trying to translate it directly from banking habits.

A third mistake is failing to record the second side of the transaction clearly. A beginner might know that cash came in but forget to ask why it came in. Was it revenue? Was it a loan? Was it owner investment? Those are very different events, even though they all increase cash. Recording only the obvious side creates incomplete and misleading books.

There is also the mistake of using the wrong account entirely. For example, when the owner takes money out of the business, some beginners record it as an expense. But owner withdrawals are not operating costs. They should go to a drawings or owner withdrawal account, not to rent, wages, or miscellaneous expense. Mixing personal withdrawals with business expenses distorts profit and makes the reports less trustworthy.

Another frequent problem is confusing **accounts payable** with **expenses**. Buying something on credit often creates both an asset or expense and a liability, depending on what was purchased. Suppose office supplies are bought on credit. The business may debit office supplies or supplies expense and credit accounts payable. Some beginners credit cash instead, even though no cash has been paid yet. That error changes the timing and tells the wrong financial story.

Beginners also sometimes mix up **accounts receivable** and **revenue**. If a service is performed on credit, the business earns revenue and creates a receivable. It does not debit revenue. Revenue is credited because it increases. The amount owed by the customer is the asset that gets debited.

There is the issue of reversal too. When reducing a liability, revenue, or equity account, beginners often instinctively credit it again because they remember that those accounts usually sit on the credit side. But a decrease moves in the opposite direction. So if accounts payable is going down because the business paid a supplier, accounts payable is debited, not credited.

Rushing is another major source of mistakes. A person sees "cash paid" and immediately credits cash without carefully asking what the other side should be. Speed without thinking leads to sloppy classification. Accounting rewards calm, methodical thinking more than fast guessing.

A stronger habit is to slow down and ask four questions:

1. What happened?
2. Which two accounts are involved?
3. Did each account increase or decrease?
4. What side records that change?

That sequence prevents a lot of beginner errors.

Some learners also become too dependent on memory tricks without understanding the logic. Memory tools can help, but if they are not connected to the accounting equation and account types, they become fragile. The real confidence comes from recognizing why accounts behave the way they do.

Finally, many beginners get discouraged too quickly. They make a few mistakes with debits and credits and conclude that accounting is not for them. That is often unnecessary. Debits and credits feel awkward mainly because they involve a new system of thought. Like learning to drive on unfamiliar roads, the first part feels tense, but repetition builds comfort.

The goal is not perfection on the first try. The goal is growing familiarity. The more you work through actual business events, the more the patterns begin to stand out. Cash received for sales. Expenses paid with cash. Inventory bought on credit. Loans received. Supplier balances paid down. Owner contributions. Owner withdrawals. The same patterns return again and again.

Once those patterns settle into place, the double-entry system stops feeling like a puzzle and starts feeling like a language you can actually speak.

CHAPTER 6

RECORDING FINANCIAL TRANSACTIONS

Every business leaves a financial trail. Each sale, payment, purchase, and loan creates a footprint that tells part of the company's financial story. When these footprints are captured accurately, the story becomes clear and useful. When they are ignored or recorded carelessly, confusion quickly takes over.

Recording financial transactions is the process that turns everyday business activity into organized financial information. Without it, financial statements would be impossible to produce, business performance would be difficult to measure, and decision-making would rely on guesswork instead of evidence.

Think of a business like a busy kitchen during dinner service. Orders are coming in, ingredients are being used, meals are going out, and staff members are working quickly to keep everything moving. If no one keeps track of what was ordered, which ingredients were used, or what customers paid for, chaos would follow. A restaurant would run out of ingredients unexpectedly, miscalculate revenue, and struggle to understand whether it was actually profitable.

Financial recording plays the same role for a business. It captures each financial action in a clear and consistent way so the bigger picture remains visible.

When transactions are recorded properly, several important things become possible. Owners can see where money is coming from and where it is going. Managers can compare income and expenses over time. Accountants can prepare financial reports that show whether the business is growing, shrinking, or simply holding steady.

Recording transactions may sound like routine work, but it is one of the most important habits in business. It builds the foundation that supports everything else in accounting.

WHY RECORDING TRANSACTIONS IS IMPORTANT

It is surprisingly easy for financial information to become unreliable if transactions are not recorded consistently. Many small business owners learn this the hard way. They may start out with a simple idea: remember the big numbers and trust memory for the rest. At first, that approach seems manageable. But as the business grows, the number of transactions multiplies quickly.

A freelancer may handle a few invoices during the first month, but within a year there may be dozens of clients, subscriptions, travel expenses, software costs, and equipment purchases. Without proper recording, the financial picture becomes blurry.

Recording transactions solves several important problems.

The first is **accuracy**. When financial events are documented immediately, there is less risk of forgetting details. Dates, amounts, and purposes remain clear because they are written down at the moment they occur.

The second is **clarity**. A record of transactions reveals patterns that would otherwise remain hidden. Business owners can see which products generate the most revenue, which expenses are increasing, and how cash moves throughout the month.

The third is **accountability**. Financial records allow businesses to verify what actually happened. If a supplier claims a payment was never received, the records can confirm whether it was paid. If a client questions an invoice, the supporting documentation is already available.

The fourth is **compliance**. Governments require businesses to maintain financial records for tax reporting and regulatory purposes. Accurate transaction recording helps ensure that financial reports reflect real activity rather than rough estimates.

Finally, recording transactions supports **decision-making**. Imagine trying to decide whether to hire another employee without knowing how much the business truly earns each month. Or deciding to expand into a new product line without knowing which products are currently profitable. Transaction records provide the raw data needed to make those choices wisely.

Many business failures can be traced not to poor ideas but to poor financial visibility. When transactions are captured carefully and consistently, the business gains a reliable mirror that reflects its financial health.

SOURCE DOCUMENTS AND FINANCIAL RECORDS

Every financial transaction begins with evidence. That evidence is known as a **source document.**

A source document is any record that proves a financial event occurred. It provides the details needed to record the transaction accurately. Without source documents, accounting would rely entirely on memory, which is unreliable and prone to mistakes.

Common source documents appear throughout everyday business activity. A few familiar examples include invoices, receipts, bank statements, purchase orders, sales tickets, and payroll records.

An **invoice** is typically issued when a business sells goods or services on credit. It lists the customer's name, the products or services provided, the amount due, and the payment terms. When a business receives an invoice from a supplier, it becomes evidence that the business owes money for goods or services received.

A **receipt** confirms that payment has already been made. When a customer buys an item and pays immediately, the receipt serves as proof of the transaction.

A **bank statement** summarizes activity within a business bank account. Deposits, withdrawals, transfers, and fees all appear there. Bank statements are particularly useful because they help verify that recorded transactions match the bank's records.

A **purchase order** is often used when a business orders goods from a supplier. It describes what was ordered and the expected price. When the goods arrive and an invoice follows, the purchase order helps confirm that everything matches.

A **sales ticket** records details of a sale at the moment it happens, especially in retail settings. Many modern point-of-sale systems generate these automatically.

Payroll records document employee wages, taxes withheld, and payments made. They are critical for maintaining accurate labor expense records.

These documents do more than prove that a transaction happened. They also provide the information needed to record it correctly. Dates, amounts, parties involved, and descriptions all come from source documents.

Businesses often keep source documents organized either physically or digitally. Some companies maintain folders for receipts and invoices, while others scan documents and store them electronically. Accounting software frequently allows documents to be attached directly to transaction records, creating a clear audit trail.

Having well-organized source documents protects the business in many ways. If financial statements are questioned by tax authorities, lenders, or investors, the documentation shows exactly how numbers were generated.

Source documents act like the supporting evidence behind every entry in the accounting system.

THE STEPS IN RECORDING TRANSACTIONS

Recording a financial transaction involves more than simply writing down an amount of money. It requires a small process that ensures the information is both accurate and meaningful.

The first step is **identifying the transaction**. Not every event in a business is a financial transaction. Conversations, ideas, and planning discussions do not belong in accounting records. The event must involve a measurable financial change.

For example, when a client agrees verbally to hire a consultant but no work has started and no payment has been arranged, nothing is recorded yet. Once the service is performed or payment terms are established, the event becomes recordable.

The second step is **analyzing the transaction**. This involves asking which accounts are affected and how they change. Does the event increase an asset? Does it create a liability? Does it generate revenue or create an expense?

Consider a small bakery purchasing ingredients with cash. The transaction increases ingredients or supplies while reducing cash. Both sides of the transaction must be recognized.

The third step is **recording the transaction in the accounting system**. This is where the double-entry system is applied. One account is debited and another is credited so that the accounting equation remains balanced.

The fourth step is **describing the transaction clearly**. A short explanation or reference to the source document helps future readers understand what happened. Without descriptions, the numbers might be correct but difficult to interpret later.

The fifth step is **verifying the information.** Reviewing the recorded entry helps ensure the correct accounts and amounts were used. Small mistakes caught early prevent larger problems later.

In practice, these steps often happen quickly. Experienced bookkeepers and accountants become comfortable recognizing transaction patterns and recording them efficiently. However, the underlying process remains the same regardless of the size of the business.

This systematic approach ensures that financial information remains organized, accurate, and ready to support reporting and analysis.

INTRODUCTION TO JOURNAL ENTRIES

Once a transaction has been identified and analyzed, it must be entered into the accounting system. The first formal record of that transaction is called a **journal entry**.

The accounting journal functions like a chronological diary of financial activity. Every transaction is recorded in the order it occurs. Each entry shows which accounts are affected, how they change, and the amount involved.

A typical journal entry includes several pieces of information. The date indicates when the transaction occurred. The accounts affected are listed, along with the amounts debited and credited. A brief description explains the purpose of the entry.

Imagine a small consulting business that receives $1,000 from a client for completed work. The journal entry would record an increase in cash and an increase in service revenue.

The entry might look like this:

Debit Cash — $1,000
Credit Service Revenue — $1,000

Description: Payment received for consulting services.

The debit indicates that cash increased, while the credit shows that revenue increased. Both sides balance, maintaining the integrity of the accounting equation.

Now imagine the same business pays $200 for internet service.

Debit Internet Expense — $200
Credit Cash — $200

Description: Payment for monthly internet service.

Again, one account increases while another decreases. The double-entry system ensures that every financial change is captured fully.

Journal entries may appear simple, but they serve a powerful purpose. They provide a detailed, time-ordered record of every financial event affecting the business. When questions arise about a particular transaction, the journal entry provides the starting point for investigation.

In modern accounting software, journal entries are often created automatically when transactions are entered through forms such as invoices, bills, or payment screens. Even so, understanding the logic behind journal entries helps users recognize what the software is doing behind the scenes.

The journal is the first step in transforming raw business activity into structured financial information.

ORGANIZING FINANCIAL INFORMATION

As transactions accumulate, the accounting system begins to fill with data. Hundreds or even thousands of entries may appear over time. Without organization, this information would be difficult to use effectively.

Accounting systems solve this problem by grouping transactions into **accounts** and summarizing activity within those accounts. The result is a clear structure that supports financial reporting.

For example, all transactions involving cash flow through the cash account. Sales revenue is recorded in revenue accounts. Rent payments appear in rent expense accounts. Equipment purchases accumulate in equipment accounts.

This organization allows financial information to be analyzed quickly. Instead of reviewing every individual transaction, business owners can examine totals within each category.

Accounting software and ledgers play an important role here. After transactions are recorded in the journal, they are posted to the appropriate accounts in the ledger. The ledger acts like a collection of folders, each dedicated to a specific type of financial activity.

Over time, the balances in these accounts form the basis of financial statements.

The **income statement** summarizes revenue and expenses to reveal profit or loss. The **balance sheet** shows assets, liabilities, and equity at a specific moment. The **cash flow statement** explains how cash moved through the business.

None of these reports would be possible without organized transaction records.

Another benefit of organized financial information is the ability to detect trends. By comparing account balances over time, businesses can observe growth patterns, rising costs, or seasonal changes in revenue.

For instance, a restaurant owner might notice that ingredient expenses increase sharply during certain months. A freelancer might see that income fluctuates depending on client demand. These insights help guide future planning.

Organized financial information also improves communication. When financial records are structured clearly, accountants, managers, investors, and lenders can understand the numbers more easily.

Ultimately, recording and organizing transactions transforms everyday business activity into meaningful financial insight. Each entry adds another piece to the puzzle, and together those pieces form a picture of how the business is performing.

When that picture is clear, decisions become more confident, risks become easier to identify, and the path forward becomes easier to navigate.

CHAPTER 7

THE GENERAL JOURNAL

Every business has a story. Some days the story is about sales and satisfied customers. Other days it is about paying suppliers, purchasing equipment, or investing in growth. Financial accounting captures this story, not through paragraphs or conversation, but through carefully recorded transactions.

The place where those financial events are first written down is called the **general journal**.

Think of the general journal as the **daily logbook of a business's financial life**. Every important financial event is recorded there in the order it happens. Just as a ship captain keeps a record of the ship's journey, the general journal keeps a chronological record of the company's financial movements.

Without the general journal, accounting would lose its structure. Transactions would appear scattered across records with no clear sequence. When questions arise—about a payment, a purchase, or a sale—there would be no reliable place to trace when and how the transaction occurred.

The general journal solves that problem. It records financial activity step by step, ensuring that every transaction leaves a clear and traceable trail.

Modern accounting software often performs this work automatically, but understanding the general journal is still essential. It reveals how accounting systems organize financial activity and how each transaction flows into the broader financial picture.

Once the general journal becomes familiar, the recording process starts to feel less mechanical and more logical. Each entry reflects a real event: money received, services provided, bills paid, or assets acquired.

WHAT THE GENERAL JOURNAL IS

The general journal is the **primary record where financial transactions are first entered into the accounting system.**

Every business activity that affects the financial position of the company eventually appears in the journal. Sales, purchases, expenses, investments, and loans all begin their accounting journey there.

The key characteristic of the general journal is **chronological order.** Transactions are recorded in the order they occur, creating a timeline of financial activity.

Imagine a small catering business that prepares meals for local events. Over the course of a week, the business may experience several financial events:

- receiving payment for a wedding catering job
- purchasing fresh ingredients
- paying a delivery driver
- buying new cooking equipment
- depositing money in the bank

Each of these events affects the business financially. Each one needs to be recorded. The general journal becomes the place where these activities are captured as they happen.

If someone later asks, "When did we buy that equipment?" or "How much did we spend on ingredients last week?" the journal can provide the answer.

Another way to understand the journal is to think of it as the **entry point of the accounting system.** After transactions are recorded there, they are later organized into accounts in the ledger, summarized in reports, and eventually presented in financial statements.

Without the journal, the accounting system would have no consistent starting point.

In traditional bookkeeping, the journal was often a physical book where entries were handwritten. Today, digital accounting systems perform the same function electronically. Whether on paper or in software, the concept remains the same: every transaction starts with a journal entry.

The journal also provides transparency. Each entry includes not only numbers but also descriptions that explain what happened. This makes it easier to understand the financial history of the business.

When accountants need to investigate a discrepancy or verify a transaction, the journal often becomes the first place they look.

THE STRUCTURE OF A JOURNAL ENTRY

A journal entry is more than just a pair of numbers. It follows a specific structure that ensures every transaction is recorded clearly and accurately.

Each entry typically contains several components that work together to describe the financial event.

The first element is the **date**. The date indicates when the transaction occurred. Recording accurate dates is essential because financial reports depend on time periods. Revenue and expenses must be recognized in the correct period for reports to be meaningful.

The next element is the **accounts involved**. Every transaction affects at least two accounts because of the double-entry system. One account will be debited, and another will be credited.

The **debit entry** appears first, followed by the **credit entry**. In traditional journal format, debit entries are aligned to the left while credit entries are slightly indented to the right.

Then comes the **amount** associated with each entry. The total of debits must always equal the total of credits.

Finally, most journal entries include a **short explanation or description**. This note provides context so that anyone reviewing the records understands the reason for the transaction.

A simple journal entry might look like this:

Date: March 5

Debit: Cash — $1,200
Credit: Service Revenue — $1,200

Description: Payment received from client for website design project.

This entry tells a complete story. On March 5, the business received cash for a service it provided. Cash increased, and revenue increased.

Another example might involve paying an expense:

Date: March 8

Debit: Office Supplies Expense — $150
Credit: Cash — $150

Description: Purchase of printer ink and office supplies.

Again, the entry shows the accounts affected, the amounts involved, and the reason for the transaction.

The structure of journal entries may appear simple, but it ensures clarity and consistency. Anyone reviewing the records can immediately understand what happened and how it affected the business financially.

RECORDING TRANSACTIONS STEP-BY-STEP

Recording transactions in the general journal follows a logical process. Instead of guessing how to record an entry, accountants and bookkeepers follow a small sequence of steps that keeps the records accurate.

The first step is **identifying the transaction**.

This means determining whether a financial event has occurred that should be recorded. For example, receiving a payment from a client qualifies as a transaction. Ordering office furniture without making payment or receiving the furniture yet may not qualify until the financial impact occurs.

Once a transaction has been identified, the next step is **analyzing its financial effect.**

This involves asking several questions:

- Which accounts are affected?
- Does each account increase or decrease?

- Are the accounts assets, liabilities, equity, revenue, or expenses?

For example, if a business pays rent, the rent expense increases and cash decreases.

The third step is **applying the debit and credit rules**.

After identifying which accounts change and how they change, the next task is deciding whether each account should be debited or credited.

In the rent example:

- Rent expense increases → debit
- Cash decreases → credit

The fourth step is **writing the journal entry**.

This includes listing the date, the accounts involved, the debit and credit amounts, and a short explanation of the transaction.

The final step is **reviewing the entry for accuracy**.

A quick review helps confirm that the debit and credit totals match and that the correct accounts were used. Even small mistakes in account selection can affect financial reports later.

Following this process keeps the recording system reliable. Instead of rushing through entries, the structured approach ensures that every financial event is captured correctly.

With practice, the process becomes natural. Experienced accountants can analyze and record transactions quickly because they recognize patterns in common business activities.

PRACTICAL EXAMPLES OF JOURNAL ENTRIES

Real-world examples make journal entries easier to understand. Let's explore several situations a small business might encounter and see how each one is recorded.

Example 1: Owner Invests Money into the Business

A business owner starts a consulting firm and deposits $8,000 into the business bank account.

Journal Entry:

Debit: Cash — $8,000
Credit: Owner's Capital — $8,000

Description: Owner investment in business.

The business now has more cash, and the owner's equity increases because the owner has invested money.

Example 2: Purchase Equipment with Cash

The consulting firm purchases a laptop for $1,200.

Journal Entry:

Debit: Equipment — $1,200
Credit: Cash — $1,200

Description: Purchase of laptop for business use.

The business gained equipment but spent cash.

Example 3: Provide Services to a Client for Cash

The firm completes a project and receives $2,000 immediately.

Journal Entry:

Debit: Cash — $2,000
Credit: Service Revenue — $2,000

Description: Payment received for consulting services.

Revenue increases because the service has been delivered.

Example 4: Provide Services on Credit

The firm completes another project but allows the client to pay later.

Journal Entry:

Debit: Accounts Receivable — $1,500
Credit: Service Revenue — $1,500

Description: Invoice issued for consulting services.

The business has earned revenue, but payment will be collected later.

Example 5: Pay Monthly Rent

The consulting firm pays office rent of $700.

Journal Entry:

Debit: Rent Expense — $700
Credit: Cash — $700

Description: Payment of monthly office rent.

The expense increases, and cash decreases.

Example 6: Pay a Supplier

The firm previously purchased office furniture on credit and now pays the supplier $900.

Journal Entry:

Debit: Accounts Payable — $900
Credit: Cash — $900

Description: Payment to furniture supplier.

The liability decreases because the debt has been settled.

These examples demonstrate how journal entries capture a wide range of financial events. Each entry records not only the numbers but also the relationship between accounts.

When hundreds of such entries accumulate over time, they form the raw data that eventually produces financial reports.

AVOIDING COMMON JOURNAL ENTRY ERRORS

Even experienced accountants occasionally make mistakes, but beginners often encounter a few predictable challenges when recording journal entries.

One common error is **recording only one side of a transaction**. Because accounting relies on the double-entry system, every transaction must include both a debit and a credit. Forgetting one side disrupts the balance of the accounting equation.

Another frequent mistake is **using the wrong account**. For example, a business owner might record a personal withdrawal as an expense rather than as an owner's drawing. This error can distort the income statement and misrepresent the profitability of the business.

There is also the issue of **confusing similar accounts**. Accounts such as accounts payable and expenses or accounts receivable and revenue may seem related but serve different purposes. Carefully identifying the nature of the transaction helps prevent this confusion.

Some errors occur when people rely too heavily on memory instead of documentation. Recording transactions without referring to source documents increases the risk of incorrect amounts or dates.

Another mistake involves **recording transactions in the wrong period**. If an expense occurs in March but is recorded in April, financial reports for both months become inaccurate.

Finally, rushing through entries without reviewing them often leads to avoidable mistakes. A quick review of each entry helps ensure that the debit and credit amounts match and that the correct accounts were selected.

Good accounting habits develop over time. Careful attention to detail, organized documentation, and consistent procedures all contribute to accurate financial records.

When journal entries are recorded correctly, they provide a reliable foundation for the rest of the accounting system. From there, transactions move into the ledger, reports begin to take shape, and the financial story of the business becomes clearer.

The general journal may appear simple at first glance, but it performs one of the most important roles in accounting: capturing the raw financial activity that drives every report and decision that follows.

CHAPTER 8

THE GENERAL LEDGER

Imagine flipping through a notebook where every financial event in a business is recorded in order. One page shows a payment from a customer, the next page shows a purchase of supplies, and the page after that records a rent payment. This running record is useful because it captures the history of what happened. But reading through dozens or hundreds of entries does not immediately tell you the answers most business owners care about. You might still be wondering how much cash is available today or how much money customers owe. The general ledger solves that problem by organizing those transactions into meaningful categories.

But a timeline alone is not enough when someone wants answers to practical questions. A business owner does not usually ask, "What happened on March 3, then March 4, then March 5?" More often, the questions sound like this: "How much cash do we have now?" "How much do customers still owe us?" "How much have we spent on rent this quarter?" "What is our current loan balance?"

The general ledger exists to answer those questions.

It takes the flow of transactions from the journal and reorganizes them by account. Instead of showing events in date order alone, it groups them into categories such as cash, rent expense, equipment, sales revenue, accounts payable, and owner's equity. This makes it possible to see the running history and current balance of each account.

A good way to picture the relationship is this: the journal is the diary, while the ledger is the filing cabinet. The diary tells the story in sequence. The filing cabinet sorts the story into labeled folders so each part can be reviewed clearly.

Without the general ledger, accounting would feel like trying to manage a business from a stack of mixed receipts and scattered notes. With the ledger, the chaos settles into order. Financial information becomes searchable, comparable, and useful. Patterns become visible. Balances can be checked. Reports can be prepared.

This is where accounting starts to feel less like recordkeeping and more like a working information system.

WHAT THE GENERAL LEDGER DOES

The general ledger is the main collection of all the accounts used by a business. It stores the effect of every recorded transaction in a way that allows each account to be tracked individually over time.

Every account has its own place in the ledger. There is a cash account, an accounts receivable account, an inventory account, a rent expense account, a service revenue account, a wages expense account, a loan payable account, and so on. Whenever a transaction affects one of these accounts, the entry is posted to that account's ledger record.

That means the general ledger performs several jobs at once.

First, it **collects information by account.** Instead of hunting through dozens of journal entries to figure out how much the business spent on utilities, you can go straight to the utilities expense account in the ledger and see every related posting in one place.

Second, it **shows movement over time.** The ledger does not just tell you the ending balance. It shows how the balance got there. You can see increases, decreases, dates, and references to the original journal entries.

Third, it **helps detect mistakes.** If a balance looks unusual, the ledger provides a trail that can be reviewed. Suppose the cash balance seems too low. The ledger allows you to examine each cash-related posting and spot possible errors or unexpected payments.

Fourth, it **supports the preparation of reports.** The income statement, balance sheet, and trial balance all depend on balances that come from the general ledger. Without the ledger, there would be no organized base from which to build these reports.

Think of a small event planning business. Over the course of a month, it receives client deposits, pays decorators, buys supplies, pays transport costs, collects final payments, and pays office rent. All of those transactions are first recorded in the journal. But when the owner wants to know total event revenue for the month, how much is still owed to suppliers, or how much cash remains in the bank, the answers come from the ledger.

The general ledger turns scattered activity into usable categories. It makes it possible to move from "a lot happened" to "here is exactly what happened in each part of the business."

In modern software, this process may happen behind the scenes. A user enters a sale, and the software automatically updates the relevant accounts in the ledger. But even when the technology handles the mechanics, understanding the ledger matters because it explains where balances come from and how accounting reports are built.

UNDERSTANDING DIFFERENT TYPES OF ACCOUNTS

A ledger is only as useful as the accounts inside it, so it helps to understand the kinds of accounts a business typically keeps.

At a broad level, ledger accounts fall into the same major categories that shape accounting itself: assets, liabilities, equity, revenue, and expenses. These categories are not just labels. They reflect the major building blocks of a business's financial life.

Asset Accounts

Asset accounts represent resources the business owns or controls. These are the tools, rights, and economic benefits the business uses to operate.

Common asset accounts include:

- Cash
- Accounts receivable
- Inventory
- Equipment
- Furniture
- Vehicles
- Prepaid insurance
- Supplies

Each asset account tracks a different type of value. Cash shows available money. Accounts receivable shows money owed by customers. Equipment shows the cost of long-term tools used in operations.

A small bakery, for example, might have asset accounts for cash, baking equipment, delivery bikes, ingredients inventory, and amounts owed by wholesale clients.

Liability Accounts

Liability accounts represent obligations the business owes to others.

Common liability accounts include:

- Accounts payable
- Loans payable
- Wages payable

- Taxes payable
- Unearned revenue

These accounts help track debts, upcoming payments, and obligations created through normal operations.

If a printing business buys paper on credit, the amount owed to the supplier goes into accounts payable. If the business borrows money from a bank to buy a machine, the balance goes into loan payable.

Equity Accounts

Equity accounts represent the owner's interest in the business.

Examples include:

- Owner's capital
- Owner's drawings or withdrawals
- Retained earnings
- Common stock, in the case of corporations

Equity grows through owner investment and profit. It shrinks through losses or owner withdrawals.

A freelance consultant who invests personal savings into the business would increase an owner's capital account. If that consultant later takes money out for personal use, the withdrawal would be recorded in a drawings account, which reduces overall equity.

Revenue Accounts

Revenue accounts record the money earned through the business's main activities.

Examples include:

- Sales revenue
- Service revenue
- Consulting revenue
- Rental income

These accounts help show how the business generates income. A salon may use service revenue for hair appointments and product sales revenue for shampoos and styling products sold in-store.

Expense Accounts

Expense accounts record the costs incurred while operating the business.

Examples include:

- Rent expense
- Wages expense

- Utilities expense
- Advertising expense
- Supplies expense
- Insurance expense
- Internet expense
- Fuel expense

Expenses matter because they reveal what the business is consuming in order to earn revenue.

A small delivery business may track fuel expense, vehicle maintenance expense, wages expense, mobile phone expense, and advertising expense. Those separate accounts help the owner see exactly where the money is going.

Why Separate Accounts Matter

Beginners sometimes wonder why businesses do not simply use one big "money in" account and one big "money out" account. The answer is that detail creates understanding.

If all income went into one generic bucket, the business would not know which service or product line was performing best. If all costs went into one expense bucket, the owner would not know whether the problem was rent, payroll, advertising, or wasteful supply spending.

Separate accounts bring clarity. They turn raw movement into meaningful categories. That clarity is what makes financial analysis possible later.

POSTING JOURNAL ENTRIES TO THE LEDGER

Posting is the process of transferring information from the journal to the appropriate accounts in the ledger.

This step is what connects the chronological record of transactions to the categorized record of account activity. Until an entry is posted, it exists in the journal but has not yet been reflected in the running balance of each affected account.

The word "posting" may sound technical, but the idea is simple. Every journal entry contains at least two affected accounts. Posting means taking each side of that entry and placing it into the correct account in the ledger.

Imagine a small design studio records the following journal entry:

Debit Cash — $2,000
Credit Service Revenue — $2,000

Description: Payment received for logo design project.

Posting this entry means:

- adding the $2,000 debit to the cash account in the ledger
- adding the $2,000 credit to the service revenue account in the ledger

Now both accounts show the effect of the transaction in their own running records.

Let us look at another example:

Debit Rent Expense — $600
Credit Cash — $600

Description: Payment of office rent.

Posting this entry means:

- adding the $600 debit to the rent expense account
- adding the $600 credit to the cash account

Over time, the cash account in the ledger will show many postings from different transactions: owner investments, customer payments, rent payments, supply purchases, loan proceeds, utility bills, and so on. The rent expense account, by contrast, will only show rent-related postings.

This is why posting matters. It allows one transaction to influence multiple categorized histories at the same time.

What Posting Looks Like in Practice

In manual systems, accountants often use ledger pages or T-accounts. Each posting includes:

- the date
- a reference to the journal entry
- the debit or credit amount
- the updated balance, in many systems

In digital systems, software performs this instantly. But the underlying logic is the same. The journal is the source. The ledger is the categorized destination.

A Simple Walkthrough

Suppose a new tutoring business records these journal entries:

1. Owner invests $5,000 cash
   Debit Cash $5,000
   Credit Owner's Capital $5,000

2. Buys a desk for $800 cash
   Debit Equipment $800
   Credit Cash $800

3. Earns $1,200 from tutoring sessions, paid in cash
   Debit Cash $1,200
   Credit Service Revenue $1,200

4. Pays internet bill of $100
   Debit Internet Expense $100
   Credit Cash $100

After posting, the ledger accounts would begin to look like this:

Cash Account

- Debit $5,000
- Credit $800
- Debit $1,200
- Credit $100

Owner's Capital

- Credit $5,000

Equipment

- Debit $800

Service Revenue

- Credit $1,200

Internet Expense

- Debit $100

From there, the running balances can be calculated.

Posting may feel repetitive, but it is one of the most important routines in accounting because it turns isolated entries into connected account histories.

TRACKING ACCOUNT BALANCES

Once journal entries are posted to the ledger, the next major benefit appears: you can track the balance of each account.

A balance is the current amount in an account after taking into consideration all increases and decreases recorded there. This is where the ledger becomes especially useful, because it shows not just one transaction, but the accumulated effect of many transactions over time.

Consider the cash account again. A business may receive money from customers, owners, and lenders. It may spend money on wages, rent, inventory, utilities, software subscriptions, and taxes. The cash account in the ledger gathers all of that movement into one place. By comparing the debits and credits, the current cash balance can be determined.

This is powerful because balance tells you where the account stands now, not just what happened once.

Running Balances

Many ledger systems use a running balance format. After each posting, the account balance is updated immediately.

For example, a cash account might look like this:

- Starting balance: $0
- Owner investment: +$10,000
- Equipment purchase: -$3,000
- Customer payment: +$2,500
- Rent payment: -$1,000

Current balance: $8,500

This running balance makes it easy to monitor changes as they happen.

Why Balances Matter

Balances help answer real business questions:

- How much cash is available right now?
- How much do customers still owe?
- How much is left on the bank loan?
- How much has been spent on marketing this month?
- What is the value of equipment recorded in the books?
- How much revenue has been earned so far this quarter?

Without account balances, those answers would require searching through every journal entry manually, which would be slow and error-prone.

Debit and Credit Balances

Each account type tends to carry a normal kind of balance.

- Assets usually carry debit balances

- Expenses usually carry debit balances
- Liabilities usually carry credit balances
- Equity usually carries credit balances
- Revenue usually carries credit balances

So if the cash account has more debits than credits, it shows a debit balance, which is normal for an asset. If accounts payable has more credits than debits, it shows a credit balance, which is normal for a liability.

If an account shows an unusual balance, that can signal a problem worth investigating. For instance, if an expense account has a credit balance when no correction entry explains it, something may have been posted incorrectly.

Example of Tracking a Balance

Suppose a small online store has the following activity in its accounts receivable account:

- Sale on credit: debit $1,000
- Another sale on credit: debit $600
- Customer payment received: credit $800

The ending accounts receivable balance is $800.

That tells the owner something useful immediately: customers still owe the business $800.

Balance tracking turns accounting from record storage into business insight.

ORGANIZING FINANCIAL DATA FOR REPORTING

The real strength of the general ledger becomes obvious when it is time to prepare reports.

A business does not create an income statement or balance sheet by digging through the journal line by line. It prepares those reports by using the balances stored in the ledger accounts. The ledger, in effect, organizes the raw financial data into a form that can be summarized and presented.

From Ledger to Trial Balance

Before formal financial statements are prepared, accountants often create a **trial balance.** This is a list of all ledger accounts and their balances at a particular date.

The trial balance serves two main purposes:

- it checks whether total debits equal total credits

- it provides the account balance list needed for report preparation

Because the ledger has already grouped transactions into accounts, preparing the trial balance becomes much easier.

From Ledger to Income Statement

Revenue and expense accounts from the ledger are used to create the income statement.

For example:

- Service Revenue
- Sales Revenue
- Rent Expense
- Wages Expense
- Utilities Expense
- Advertising Expense

These balances are combined to show whether the business made a profit or a loss during the period.

Without the ledger, it would be difficult to know total rent expense or total service revenue. With the ledger, those amounts are already organized and ready.

From Ledger to Balance Sheet

Asset, liability, and equity accounts from the ledger are used to create the balance sheet.

Examples include:

- Cash
- Accounts Receivable
- Inventory
- Equipment
- Accounts Payable
- Loan Payable
- Owner's Capital

These balances provide a snapshot of the business's financial position at a specific moment.

Again, the ledger makes this possible by maintaining updated balances in each account.

Why Organization Changes Everything

A business owner often begins by thinking accounting is mostly about tracking money. Over time, it becomes clear that accounting is really about organizing information so it can be used.

That organization helps with:

- reporting profit accurately
- monitoring cash and debt
- comparing months or years
- preparing taxes
- supporting loan applications
- answering investor questions
- spotting financial problems early

Imagine a small furniture workshop trying to apply for a business loan. The lender asks for recent financial statements. Those reports cannot be built from memory or a pile of receipts. They come from organized ledger data that has been recorded and maintained properly over time.

Or imagine a freelance videographer reviewing the year's performance. The ledger reveals total revenue, editing software costs, travel expenses, equipment purchases, and unpaid client balances. It gives shape to the year. It turns activity into understanding.

That is what the general ledger really does. It takes the messiness of day-to-day business life and arranges it into something readable, traceable, and useful. It does not make decisions on behalf of the business, but it gives decision-makers something solid to stand on.

Once financial data is organized well, the business no longer has to rely on instinct alone. It can look at the numbers, ask better questions, and move forward with far more confidence.

CHAPTER 9

TRIAL BALANCE AND ACCURACY

A business can record transactions every day, post them to the ledger, and still end up with financial confusion if the numbers are not checked carefully along the way. That is where the trial balance comes in. It is one of the simplest tools in accounting, yet it performs an essential job. It helps confirm that the bookkeeping process is still standing on solid ground before financial statements are prepared.

Think of the trial balance as a checkpoint rather than a destination. It does not tell the whole financial story on its own, but it tells you whether the story has been organized properly so far. If the records are in order, the total debits and total credits should match. If they do not, it is a warning sign. Somewhere in the process, something has gone wrong.

This matters because accounting is built on structure. A single missed digit, a posting to the wrong side of an account, or a skipped ledger entry can quietly distort the financial picture. Those small errors may not look dramatic in isolation, but once they flow into reports, they can mislead business owners, managers, lenders, and investors.

The trial balance gives accounting its pause-and-check moment. It is the point where the books are asked a simple but important question: do the numbers still hold together?

For beginners, the trial balance is especially useful because it turns abstract accounting logic into something visible. You can actually see the list of account balances, compare the totals, and judge whether the system remains in balance. It is one of the clearest reminders that accounting is not random recordkeeping. It is an ordered system, and that system depends on accuracy.

WHAT A TRIAL BALANCE IS

A trial balance is a list of all the accounts in the general ledger and their balances at a specific point in time. These balances are separated into debit balances and credit balances. The purpose is straightforward: to check whether total debits equal total credits.

That may sound modest, but it is incredibly important.

Every recorded transaction follows the double-entry system. That means every debit should have an equal credit somewhere in the records. Because of that structure, the total of all debit balances in the ledger should match the total of all credit balances. When a trial balance is prepared, it reveals whether that basic mathematical relationship still holds.

A trial balance usually includes accounts such as:

- Cash
- Accounts receivable
- Inventory
- Equipment
- Accounts payable
- Loan payable
- Owner's capital
- Sales revenue
- Rent expense
- Utilities expense
- Wages expense

Each account appears with its ending balance. If the account has a debit balance, the amount is placed in the debit column. If it has a credit balance, the amount is placed in the credit column.

Here is the important distinction: a trial balance is not the same thing as a financial statement.

It does not organize accounts into polished report sections the way an income statement or balance sheet does. It is more like a working document. Its job is to present ledger balances in a form that makes checking and preparation easier.

You can think of it as the accounting equivalent of laying all your tools out on a table before starting a repair job. Everything is visible. Everything is in one place. And before moving forward, you can quickly see whether anything is obviously missing or out of place.

For a small business owner, the trial balance can also be surprisingly revealing. It offers a compressed view of the business's accounting structure. Even without preparing the final reports, you can start to see how much cash is available, how much is owed, how much revenue has been earned, and which expenses are piling up.

The beauty of the trial balance is that it is simple enough to prepare once the ledger is complete, but meaningful enough to catch problems before they spread further.

PREPARING A TRIAL BALANCE

Preparing a trial balance is a fairly mechanical process, but it rewards careful attention. The quality of the result depends entirely on the quality of the underlying ledger balances.

The first step is to gather the ending balance of every account from the general ledger. Each account should already reflect all postings made during the period being examined. That means journal entries have been recorded, posted correctly, and updated so the current balance of each account is available.

Once those balances are ready, the accounts are listed in a trial balance format. Businesses often arrange them in a familiar order, starting with assets, then liabilities, then equity, followed by revenue and expenses. The exact presentation can vary, but the key requirement is that every relevant account balance appears once, and only once.

Each balance is entered into either the debit column or the credit column, depending on its nature.

For example:

- Cash usually appears as a debit balance

- Accounts receivable usually appears as a debit balance
- Equipment usually appears as a debit balance
- Accounts payable usually appears as a credit balance
- Owner's capital usually appears as a credit balance
- Revenue usually appears as a credit balance
- Expenses usually appear as debit balances

After all balances are listed, the debit column is totaled and the credit column is totaled. If the books are in order, those two totals should be equal.

Let us walk through a simple example.

Imagine a tutoring business with the following ledger balances at the end of the month:

- Cash: $4,500 debit
- Accounts Receivable: $800 debit
- Equipment: $1,200 debit
- Accounts Payable: $600 credit
- Owner's Capital: $3,500 credit
- Service Revenue: $2,000 credit
- Rent Expense: $700 debit
- Internet Expense: $100 debit
- Supplies Expense: $300 debit

Now list them in a trial balance:

ACCOUNT	DEBIT	CREDIT
Cash	4,500	
Accounts Receivable	800	
Equipment	1,200	
Accounts Payable		600
Owner's Capital		3,500
Service Revenue		2,000
Rent Expense	700	
Internet Expense	100	
Supplies Expense	300	
Total	**7,600**	**6,100**

This does **not** balance, which means something is wrong. Maybe an account is missing. Maybe a balance was copied incorrectly. Maybe a ledger posting error happened earlier. The trial balance has done its job by flagging the issue.

Now suppose there was also a wages expense balance of $1,500 debit that had been omitted. Add it:

ACCOUNT	DEBIT	CREDIT
Cash	4,500	
Accounts Receivable	800	
Equipment	1,200	
Account Payable		600
Owner's Capital		3,500
Service Revenue		2,000
Rent Expense	700	
Internet	100	

Expense		
Supplies Expense	300	
Wage Expense	1,500	
Total	**9,100**	**6,100**

Still not balanced. That means the problem is not fully resolved. The business would need to continue checking the ledger balances and postings.

This example shows something useful: preparing a trial balance is not only about formatting a list. It is about creating a test. The moment the totals fail to match, the accountant knows it is time to investigate.

In real practice, once the trial balance is successfully prepared, it becomes the foundation for later accounting work, including adjustments and financial statement preparation.

WHY TRIAL BALANCES MUST ALWAYS BALANCE

The reason a trial balance must balance goes back to the foundation of double-entry accounting. Every transaction has two sides, and the total debits recorded must always equal the total credits recorded.

That principle does not disappear once transactions leave the journal. It travels all the way through the ledger and into the trial balance.

If a business records a $1,000 cash sale, cash is debited and revenue is credited by the same amount. If it buys equipment for cash, equipment is debited and cash is credited by the same amount. If it takes a loan, cash is debited and loan payable is credited. Every properly recorded transaction preserves the equality of debits and credits.

Because the ledger is built from these transactions, the total of all ledger debit balances should match the total of all ledger credit balances. The trial balance is simply the visible test of that truth.

So when a trial balance does not balance, it suggests one of several things:

- A journal entry was not balanced correctly
- A ledger posting was made to one side but not the other
- A number was copied incorrectly
- An account balance was placed in the wrong column
- An account was omitted entirely

Balancing matters because it is one of the fastest ways to confirm that the accounting system still reflects internal consistency.

But there is an important caution here. A balanced trial balance does **not** guarantee that everything is correct.

This is a point beginners often miss. A trial balance can balance even when certain types of errors still exist. For example:

- A transaction may have been posted to the wrong account but with the correct amount on each side
- A transaction may have been omitted completely
- Two equal and opposite errors may cancel each other out

- An entry may have been recorded with the wrong amount on both the debit and credit side

In those situations, the trial balance will still balance, even though the records contain mistakes.

So the trial balance is powerful, but not magical. It confirms that the debit-credit structure holds. It does not confirm that every account choice or amount is logically correct.

Still, that structural check is vital. It is far better to catch an imbalance before financial statements are created than after misleading reports have already gone out to owners, banks, or investors.

In a way, the trial balance acts like a scale. If the scale tips heavily to one side, something is clearly off. If it balances, that is encouraging, but you still need to confirm that what is sitting on the scale actually belongs there.

IDENTIFYING AND CORRECTING ERRORS

When a trial balance does not balance, the next task is not panic. It is investigation.

Accounting errors are common, especially in manual systems or early learning stages. What matters is developing a calm, methodical approach to finding them.

The first step is to recheck the arithmetic. Sometimes the problem is simple. A column may have been added incorrectly. A single number may have been copied as 540 instead of 450. These are not conceptual errors. They are mechanical ones, and they are often the easiest to fix.

The second step is to verify that every ledger account balance was included in the trial balance. Missing accounts are a common source of imbalance. An expense account, revenue account, or payable account may have been left out by accident.

The third step is to confirm that each balance was entered into the correct column. An asset or expense account accidentally placed in the credit column will throw off the total. So will a liability or revenue account placed in the debit column.

The fourth step is to review the ledger balances themselves. A trial balance can only be correct if the ledger is correct. If one ledger account balance was computed incorrectly, the trial balance will inherit that mistake.

The fifth step is to go back to the journal entries and posting process. Look for things like:

- One side of an entry posted without the other
- A debit posted as a credit
- A posting to the wrong account
- A transposed number, such as 64 instead of 46

A useful clue comes from the size of the difference between total debits and credits. Suppose the difference is divisible by 9. That can sometimes suggest a transposition error, where digits were reversed. It is not a perfect rule, but it can point the search in a useful direction.

Let us look at a practical example.

A small photography business prepares a trial balance and finds that the debit total is $9,250 while the credit total is $8,950. There is a $300 difference.

The owner reviews the process and discovers that a $300 supplies expense was entered in the ledger correctly but never included in the trial balance. Once that account is added, the totals match.

Here is another example.

A business posts a journal entry for paying rent:

Debit Rent Expense $700
Credit Cash $700

But when posting to the ledger, the cash account is mistakenly credited with $70 instead of $700. The trial balance will not balance because the debit side exceeds the credit side by $630. The fix is to correct the cash ledger posting.

Now consider a balanced-but-wrong situation. A business buys office chairs for $500 cash but mistakenly records:

Debit Supplies Expense $500
Credit Cash $500

The trial balance will balance. But the business has recorded the purchase in the wrong account. It should likely have gone to furniture or equipment, not supplies expense. This shows why accounting review cannot stop at "the columns match." Judgment matters too.

When correcting errors, accountants often use adjusting or correcting journal entries rather than simply erasing past records, especially in formal systems. This preserves the audit trail and keeps the books transparent.

The main lesson is that accuracy is not about perfection from the start. It is about having a process strong enough to detect, investigate, and correct mistakes before they damage the usefulness of the records.

THE ROLE OF ACCURACY IN FINANCIAL REPORTING

Financial reporting depends on trust. A balance sheet is only useful if the balances are real. An income statement is only meaningful if revenue and expenses were recorded correctly. A cash flow statement only helps decision-making if cash movements were captured accurately.

That is why accuracy is not a minor accounting preference. It is the difference between information that helps and information that misleads.

Imagine a small business owner reviewing the monthly profit figure. If expenses were understated because several bills were missed, profit will appear stronger than it really is. The owner may decide to hire staff, increase spending, or take money out of the business based on a false sense of financial strength.

Or picture a lender examining a loan application. If liabilities were recorded incorrectly, the business may seem less risky than it actually is. That could lead to poor lending decisions and serious consequences later.

Accuracy also matters for taxes, investor communication, budgeting, and long-term planning. Businesses make real decisions based on accounting numbers. When those numbers are wrong, the decisions built on them are weakened.

This is why accounting includes checkpoints like the trial balance. They are not there to make the process feel formal or tedious. They exist because businesses need dependable numbers.

Accurate reporting supports:

- Better decision-making
- Fair tax reporting
- Stronger lender and investor confidence
- Clearer performance measurement
- Better cash and cost control
- Reduced risk of fraud or carelessness

For beginners, it is worth understanding that accuracy is not only about getting the arithmetic right. It also means:

- Using the correct accounts
- Recording transactions in the correct period
- Posting amounts fully and carefully
- Preserving supporting documents
- Reviewing unusual balances
- Questioning numbers that do not make business sense

A trial balance is part of that discipline. It encourages a mindset that says, "Before moving forward, let's make sure the foundation is sound."

That mindset is valuable whether the business is a one-person freelance service or a large organization with a full accounting department.

When accounting is accurate, financial reports become more than paperwork. They become reliable tools for understanding reality. And in business, seeing reality clearly is one of the greatest advantages a person can have.

CHAPTER 10

ADJUSTING ENTRIES AND ACCOUNTING PERIODS

A business does not stop and restart neatly every time the calendar flips to a new month. Rent keeps running. Employees keep working. subscriptions continue. equipment wears down. Clients may receive a service today and pay next month. A business might pay for insurance now and use that coverage over the next twelve months. Real business life flows continuously, but financial reporting has to pause at specific dates and say, "This is what belongs to this period, and this is what belongs to the next one."

That is where adjusting entries come in.

Adjusting entries are the quiet clean-up crew of accounting. They make sure the numbers reflect reality as closely as possible at the end of an accounting period. Without them, financial statements can look neat on the surface while quietly telling the wrong story underneath. Revenue may be missing. Expenses may be understated. Assets may be overstated. Liabilities may be invisible. Profit may look stronger or weaker than it really is.

This matters because timing matters in accounting.

It is not enough to know that money was received or paid. The business also needs to know **when value was earned** and **when costs were actually incurred**. That timing is what allows financial statements to be useful. A business owner looking at a monthly income statement wants to know what that month truly produced and what that month truly consumed, not just what happened to pass through the bank account.

Think of accounting periods like snapshots. If you take a photo of a business on the last day of the month, the picture should include all the income earned up to that date and all the costs connected to that same period, even if cash has not yet moved for every item. Adjusting entries sharpen that picture.

They are not about changing reality. They are about recording it properly.

WHY ADJUSTMENTS ARE NECESSARY

If accounting only recorded transactions when cash changed hands, many financial reports would be misleading.

Imagine a web designer who completes a project in March but gets paid in April. If the business waits until April to record the revenue, March will look weaker than it really was, and April will look stronger than it should. The work belonged to March, even though the cash arrived later.

Now imagine a business that pays one year of insurance in January. If the full payment is recorded as January expense, that month will look overloaded with cost, while the following eleven months will benefit from insurance coverage without showing any related expense. That does not reflect the real pattern of benefit.

This is the problem adjusting entries are designed to solve.

They help accounting follow a more truthful principle: record income when it is earned and record expenses when they are incurred or used up. This is closely tied to accrual accounting, which aims to match financial activity to the correct time period.

Businesses prepare financial statements for specific periods:

- monthly
- quarterly
- yearly

Each report needs boundaries. If those boundaries are not respected, the numbers lose meaning.

Adjustments are necessary for several reasons.

First, they help **match revenue with the period in which it was earned**. A business may provide services before cash is received. If that earned value is ignored, the income statement understates performance.

Second, they help **match expenses with the period in which they helped generate revenue**. Costs such as utilities, wages, insurance, and depreciation often relate to a period even if payment timing does not line up perfectly.

Third, they help present a **more accurate balance sheet**. Assets and liabilities should reflect what the business truly owns and owes at the reporting date. If adjustments are skipped, balances can become distorted. For example, prepaid insurance might stay too high, or unpaid wages might never appear as a liability.

Fourth, they support **credible decision-making**. Owners, managers, lenders, and investors rely on financial statements to judge performance and financial health. If those reports are not adjusted properly, decisions may be based on false signals.

You can think of adjusting entries as the final tidying-up before the numbers are presented to the world. They make sure unfinished business is not ignored and future benefits are not treated as if they have already been fully consumed.

Without adjustments, accounting periods blur together. With them, each period tells a cleaner and more honest story.

ACCRUED REVENUES AND EXPENSES

Some of the most important adjustments involve items that have already been earned or incurred, even though cash has not yet changed hands. These are called **accruals**.

Accruals bring accounting closer to the real economic activity of the business. They recognize that value can be created before payment arrives, and obligations can arise before the bill is paid.

Accrued Revenue

Accrued revenue is revenue the business has earned but has not yet received in cash and may not yet have formally billed.

Imagine a consulting firm that completes a week-long assignment on March 30, with the client scheduled to pay on April 10. From a business point of view, the work has already been done in March. The revenue belongs to March, not April.

If the books are closed on March 31 without adjustment, March revenue is understated and assets are understated, because the business has a right to receive payment.

To fix this, the business records an adjusting entry:

- **Debit Accounts Receivable**
- **Credit Revenue**

This entry says, in effect, "We earned this, and we are owed this."

A simple example:

A business completes services worth $1,200 before month-end but has not yet billed the client.

Adjusting entry:

- Debit Accounts Receivable $1,200
- Credit Service Revenue $1,200

Now the income statement includes the earned revenue, and the balance sheet shows that customers owe the business money.

Accrued revenue is common in service businesses, consulting work, legal work, tutoring, maintenance contracts, and any setup where work may be completed before billing or collection.

Accrued Expenses

Accrued expenses are costs the business has already incurred but has not yet paid.

This is extremely common in everyday operations.

A classic example is wages. Employees may work during the last few days of the month, but payroll may not be processed until the next month. Even though cash has not yet gone out, the business has already consumed the labor. The cost belongs to the current period.

Suppose employees have earned $900 by month-end, but payment will happen next week.

Adjusting entry:

- Debit Wages Expense $900
- Credit Wages Payable $900

That entry records the expense in the correct period and also shows a liability, because the business owes the employees that money.

Another common example is utilities. A business may use electricity throughout the month but receive the bill after the month ends. The business still consumed the service during the month, so some amount should be recognized.

Suppose estimated electricity cost for the month is $250, but the bill will arrive later.

Adjusting entry:

- Debit Utilities Expense $250
- Credit Utilities Payable $250

Accrued expenses can also include:

- interest on loans
- taxes owed but not yet paid
- professional fees earned by outside providers
- commissions owed

Why Accruals Matter

Accruals keep the income statement honest. They stop businesses from pretending that unbilled work does not count yet or that unpaid costs do not exist yet.

Without accrued revenues, performance can look weaker than it is. Without accrued expenses, profit can look stronger than it is.

Both errors can lead to poor decisions.

Accruals remind us that accounting is not only about cash. It is about economic reality during a period.

PREPAID EXPENSES AND UNEARNED REVENUE

Not all adjustments deal with missing amounts. Some deal with amounts that were recorded too early.

This often happens when cash changes hands before the related benefit is fully used or before the related revenue is fully earned. Two common examples are prepaid expenses and unearned revenue.

Prepaid Expenses

A prepaid expense is a payment made in advance for something the business will use over time.

At the moment of payment, it might feel natural to record the full amount as an expense. After all, cash left the bank. But if the benefit stretches into future periods, recording it all at once would distort the numbers.

Common prepaid expenses include:

- insurance
- rent paid in advance
- software subscriptions
- maintenance contracts
- advertising packages paid ahead of time

Let us say a business pays $2,400 for a 12-month insurance policy starting January 1.

At first, that payment should be recorded as an asset, often called Prepaid Insurance, because the business now holds a future benefit. It has paid for coverage it has not yet fully used.

Initial entry:

- Debit Prepaid Insurance $2,400
- Credit Cash $2,400

After one month, one-twelfth of that benefit has been used. That means $200 should move from asset to expense.

Adjusting entry at month-end:

- Debit Insurance Expense $200
- Credit Prepaid Insurance $200

Now the financial statements reflect reality more clearly:

- one month of insurance has been consumed as expense
- the remaining eleven months still sit on the balance sheet as future benefit

This pattern continues period by period until the prepaid asset is used up.

Unearned Revenue

Unearned revenue, sometimes called deferred revenue, is the opposite kind of timing issue. Here, the business receives cash before it has delivered the goods or services.

At first, that cash is not yet earned revenue. It is an obligation.

Imagine a fitness coach who receives $600 in advance for a three-month coaching package. On the day the payment arrives, the coach has cash, yes, but has not yet earned all of it. The business owes the client future sessions.

Initial entry:

- Debit Cash $600
- Credit Unearned Revenue $600

As the coach delivers sessions over time, the liability decreases and revenue is recognized gradually.

Suppose one month of service has been delivered, representing $200 of the package.

Adjusting entry:

- Debit Unearned Revenue $200
- Credit Service Revenue $200

That entry says, "Part of what was owed has now been delivered, so part of the liability becomes earned revenue."

Unearned revenue is common in businesses such as:

- subscription services
- coaching programs
- annual memberships
- magazine subscriptions
- prepaid maintenance plans
- event deposits
- gift cards in some settings

Why These Adjustments Matter

Prepaid expenses and unearned revenue both protect the timing of financial statements.

Without adjusting prepaid expenses, assets may stay too high and expenses too low. Without adjusting unearned revenue, liabilities may stay too high and revenue too low, or worse, revenue may be recognized too early.

These adjustments keep businesses from confusing cash timing with performance timing. Just because money moved does not mean the full expense or full revenue belongs to the current period.

That distinction is one of the marks of stronger accounting.

DEPRECIATION EXPLAINED SIMPLY

Depreciation is one of those accounting words that sounds heavier than it really is.

At its heart, depreciation is just a method of spreading the cost of a long-term asset over the period it is expected to be useful.

When a business buys something like equipment, furniture, a delivery van, or machinery, it usually gets value from that asset for more than one accounting period. Because of that, accounting does not usually treat the whole purchase price as an expense immediately. Instead, the asset is recorded on the balance sheet, and part of its cost is recognized as expense over time.

Think of buying a commercial oven for a bakery. If the oven costs $6,000 and is expected to be useful for six years, it would not make sense to dump the full $6,000 into one month's expense if the oven will help produce revenue for years. That would make the first month look unfairly expensive and later periods look artificially better.

Depreciation solves that mismatch.

The Basic Idea

Depreciation recognizes that long-term assets are gradually used up, worn down, or consumed in service over time.

It is not necessarily about market value. A delivery van may lose resale value, yes, but accounting depreciation is mainly about allocating cost across useful periods.

A Simple Straight-Line Example

The easiest method for beginners is straight-line depreciation.

Suppose a business buys office furniture for $3,000 and expects to use it for 5 years, with no salvage value at the end.

Annual depreciation: $3,000 ÷ 5 = $600 per year

If the business prepares monthly statements, monthly depreciation would be: $600 ÷ 12 = $50 per month

Adjusting entry each month:

- Debit Depreciation Expense $50
- Credit Accumulated Depreciation $50

This entry is interesting because it does not reduce the asset account directly. Instead, it credits a related account called **Accumulated Depreciation**, which is a contra-asset account. It sits alongside the asset and shows how much of the asset's cost has been allocated so far.

So if furniture cost is $3,000 and accumulated depreciation is $500, the net book value is $2,500.

Why Depreciation Matters

Depreciation matters because it:

- matches asset cost to the periods benefiting from its use
- prevents profit from being distorted
- gives a more realistic picture of asset value over time
- supports better long-term cost awareness

Suppose a delivery business buys a motorcycle for $2,400 and records the full amount as expense immediately. That month's profit may collapse unnecessarily, even though the motorcycle will help generate income for years. Depreciation spreads the cost more fairly.

Common Assets That Depreciate

Businesses often depreciate:

- vehicles
- office furniture
- computers
- machinery
- tools
- equipment
- buildings, in many cases excluding land

Land is usually not depreciated because it is generally considered to have an unlimited useful life.

A Simple Way to Think About It

A useful analogy is a candle. If you buy a candle and burn it over several evenings, you would not say all the light belonged to the first evening. The candle's usefulness is gradually consumed. Depreciation is accounting's way of recognizing that slow consumption for long-term business assets.

Once beginners grasp that idea, depreciation becomes much less intimidating. It is simply cost allocation over time.

PREPARING ACCOUNTS FOR FINANCIAL STATEMENTS

After adjustments are recorded, the accounts are much closer to the truth the financial statements need to show.

This stage is where all the earlier work starts to come together. Transactions were recorded. Journal entries were posted. Trial balances were checked. Adjustments were made for timing and accuracy. Now the accounts are prepared for presentation.

Preparing the Books for Final Reporting

Financial statements are only as good as the balances that feed into them.

If wages payable is missing, liabilities are understated. If prepaid insurance was never adjusted, assets are overstated and expenses understated.

If earned but unbilled revenue was ignored, both revenue and receivables are understated. If depreciation was skipped, profit may look too high and assets may look too strong.

Adjusting entries prepare the accounts so the final reports reflect the correct period as closely as possible.

The Adjusted Trial Balance

After adjustments are made, accountants often prepare an **adjusted trial balance**. This is similar to the earlier trial balance, but now it includes the updated balances after all end-of-period adjustments.

The adjusted trial balance becomes the main source for preparing:

- the income statement
- the balance sheet
- and later, depending on the system, other reports such as cash flow support schedules

This document acts like the final organized checklist before formal reporting.

Moving Toward the Income Statement

The income statement uses revenue and expense accounts.

After adjustments, these balances should now reflect:

- all revenue earned in the period
- all expenses incurred in the period

For example, revenue may now include accrued service income, and expenses may now include wages owed, utilities used, insurance consumed, and depreciation.

That leads to a more meaningful profit figure.

Moving Toward the Balance Sheet

The balance sheet uses assets, liabilities, and equity accounts.

After adjustments, these balances should now reflect:

- receivables that truly exist
- payables that truly exist
- prepaid amounts that still represent future benefit
- unearned revenue that still represents remaining obligation

- long-term assets shown alongside accumulated depreciation
- equity updated through the effects of revenue and expenses

This gives a clearer snapshot of financial position at the reporting date.

A Mini Example

Imagine a small tutoring business at month-end.

Before adjustments:

- Cash: $4,000
- Accounts Receivable: $0
- Prepaid Insurance: $1,200
- Unearned Revenue: $600
- Revenue: $3,000
- Wages Expense: $900

Now suppose the following adjustments are needed:

- $500 of services were performed but not yet billed
- one month of insurance, $100, has been used
- $200 of prepaid tutoring sessions have now been delivered
- $300 of wages are owed but unpaid

Adjusted entries:

1. Debit Accounts Receivable $500
   Credit Revenue $500

2. Debit Insurance Expense $100
   Credit Prepaid Insurance $100

3. Debit Unearned Revenue $200
   Credit Revenue $200

4. Debit Wages Expense $300
   Credit Wages Payable $300

Now the numbers tell a richer and more accurate story:

- revenue rises to include what was actually earned
- insurance expense reflects what was used
- unearned revenue falls to reflect what has now been delivered
- liabilities include wages the business truly owes

That is the power of preparing accounts properly before reporting.

The Bigger Purpose

This part of accounting is where patience pays off. Adjustments are not flashy, but they are one of the reasons financial accounting can be trusted at all. They take the rough edges off the raw records and help shape them into something fair, timely, and useful.

For a business owner, that means better decisions. For a lender, it means better assessment. For an investor, it means more reliable insight. For anyone trying to understand the business, it means the reports are less likely to mislead.

When accounts are adjusted well, the financial statements stop being just a pile of numbers arranged in columns. They become a more faithful picture of what the business actually earned, used, owned, and owed during the period.

CHAPTER 11

INTRODUCTION TO FINANCIAL STATEMENTS

At some point, every business reaches a moment where scattered numbers are no longer enough. A list of receipts will not tell you whether the business is healthy. A bank balance alone will not tell you whether the company is profitable. A pile of invoices cannot easily explain whether customers are paying on time, whether debts are growing, or whether the business is building real value.

That is why financial statements matter.

Financial statements take the raw activity of a business and turn it into a readable picture. They do not capture every detail of daily operations, but they capture the essentials. They show what the business earned, what it spent, what it owns, what it owes, and how cash moved. In other words, they help translate business activity into financial understanding.

For many beginners, financial statements look intimidating at first glance because they appear formal and number-heavy. But underneath the layout, the ideas are surprisingly practical. These reports are not created to impress accountants. They exist to answer very human business questions.

Is the business actually making money?
Can it pay its bills?
Is it growing stronger or becoming stretched?
Are the numbers healthy enough to support expansion, borrowing, or hiring?

Financial statements help answer those questions with structure instead of guesswork.

A useful way to think about them is this: if a business were a person, financial statements would be something like a health check. One report would show performance over time, another would show the current condition, and another would show how money has been flowing through the system. None of them tells the whole story alone, but together they reveal a lot.

Once these reports begin to make sense, accounting starts to feel far more practical. Instead of being a subject filled with abstract terms, it becomes a way of seeing clearly.

THE PURPOSE OF FINANCIAL STATEMENTS

The main purpose of financial statements is simple: they organize financial information so people can understand the condition and performance of a business.

Without financial statements, important information stays buried inside journals, ledgers, receipts, invoices, payroll records, and bank transactions. That information exists, but it is too scattered to be useful in a clear, timely way. Financial statements gather the important parts and present them in a structured format.

They serve as a kind of summary, but not a vague one. A good financial statement is a carefully arranged summary that helps people see what matters.

Business owners use financial statements to understand whether the business is profitable, stable, and manageable. Managers use them to guide planning, control costs, and monitor performance. Lenders use them to judge whether a business can repay a loan. Investors use them to decide whether a company seems worth backing. Tax authorities use them as part of financial verification. Even employees in leadership roles may rely on them to understand how their department or company is doing.

The reports are not just useful for outsiders. They are often most useful for the people inside the business who need to make decisions every day.

Imagine a small cleaning company with growing demand. The owner is considering hiring two new workers and buying another vehicle. That sounds promising, but optimism alone is not enough. The owner needs to know whether current profit levels are strong enough, whether cash reserves can support expansion, and whether existing debts are already too heavy. Financial statements help answer those questions before the decision is made.

They also create accountability. Once numbers are formally reported, it becomes harder to hide behind vague impressions. A business owner may feel like the company is doing well because customers are busy and sales are happening. But if the income statement shows weak profit and the balance sheet shows rising debt, the mood of the business may not match the financial reality.

That is one of the quiet strengths of financial statements. They force clarity.

They also allow comparison. A business can compare this month to last month, this year to last year, or actual results to budgeted expectations. Those comparisons help spot trends, strengths, and warning signs.

At their best, financial statements help a business move from instinct to evidence. Instinct still matters in business, but evidence sharpens it.

THE THREE CORE FINANCIAL REPORTS

Most beginner accounting work eventually leads toward three main reports. These are the backbone of financial reporting:

- the income statement
- the balance sheet
- the cash flow statement

Each one answers a different question.

The income statement answers: **Did the business make a profit?**
The balance sheet answers: **What does the business own and owe right now?**
The cash flow statement answers: **How did cash move through the business?**

Each report looks at the business from a different angle, much like three camera shots of the same scene.

The income statement focuses on performance over a period of time. It shows revenue, expenses, and the resulting profit or loss. If a business earned more than it spent, it reports profit. If expenses were higher than revenue, it reports a loss. This statement is especially useful because it shows whether the business model is producing enough income to cover costs.

The balance sheet is different. It is not about a stretch of time in the same way. It is more like a snapshot taken at a specific date. It lists assets, liabilities, and equity. It shows what the business has, what it owes, and what belongs to the owner or owners after debts are considered. If the income statement tells you how the business performed, the balance sheet tells you where the business stands.

Then there is the cash flow statement. This one often becomes a favorite once people understand it, because cash has a way of cutting through illusions. A business may report profit and still feel constant cash pressure. Another business may not look impressive on paper at first glance but may be managing cash quite well. The cash flow statement explains where cash came from and where it went, usually grouped into operating, investing, and financing activities.

Each report matters on its own, but none should be treated as complete in isolation.

A profitable business can still have poor cash flow. A business with strong assets can still be struggling with too much debt. A cash-rich business can still be hiding weak profitability.

That is why serious financial understanding comes from reading the three together rather than treating one report as the whole truth.

HOW FINANCIAL STATEMENTS WORK TOGETHER

One of the most important things beginners can learn is that financial statements are connected. They are not separate islands. They speak to each other.

Once that connection becomes clear, the reports start to feel much more logical.

Start with profit. Profit is measured on the income statement. If a business earns revenue and controls its expenses well, it reports a positive result. That result does not simply disappear once the income statement is prepared. It affects equity on the balance sheet. Profit increases the owner's interest in the business, assuming it is retained rather than withdrawn.

Now think about cash. A business might report strong revenue on the income statement, but if many customers have not paid yet, the cash may not have arrived. That unpaid amount may appear as accounts receivable on the balance sheet. So the income statement may say value was earned, while the balance sheet shows that some of that value is still waiting to be collected.

Then the cash flow statement steps in and explains what actually happened with cash. It helps bridge the gap between profit and cash reality. This is important because many beginners assume that profit and cash should always match. In real life, they often do not. The cash flow statement shows why.

Let us take a simple example.

A business earns $10,000 in revenue during the month and reports $2,500 in profit after expenses. That looks encouraging on the income statement. But suppose $4,000 of the revenue has not yet been collected from customers. On the balance sheet, that amount shows up as accounts receivable. Meanwhile, suppose the business also bought new equipment, which increased assets but used cash. The cash flow statement would reveal those movements, helping explain why the bank balance may not have risen by the same amount as profit.

This connection is why good financial reading involves moving back and forth between reports.

You may notice rising profit and ask whether cash is also improving.
You may notice strong assets and ask whether they are financed by healthy equity or heavy debt.
You may notice strong cash and ask whether it came from operations or from borrowing.

The reports work best as a conversation, not as isolated pieces of paper.

There is also a deeper comfort in this connection. It means the financial story is not random. The reports are built from the same accounting system and the same underlying transactions. They show different views of the same business reality.

That is why learning one report makes the next one easier. The logic carries through.

WHY BUSINESSES RELY ON FINANCIAL REPORTS

Businesses rely on financial reports for the same reason pilots rely on instruments. You cannot safely guide something important using instinct alone.

A business owner may be hardworking, experienced, and deeply involved in daily operations, but daily effort is not the same thing as financial clarity. A busy business is not always a healthy business. Strong sales are not always strong profit. A full schedule is not always a stable future.

Financial reports cut through appearances.

They help owners and managers answer practical questions such as:

- Are we making enough profit to justify the effort?
- Are expenses increasing too quickly?
- Can we afford to hire more staff?
- Do we have enough cash to cover the next few months?

- Are customers paying on time?
- Is debt becoming a problem?
- Are we financially ready to expand?

Without reports, these questions are often answered emotionally. With reports, they can be answered with evidence.

Banks rely on financial reports before approving loans because lenders want to see whether a business can reasonably repay what it borrows. Investors rely on them because they want to know whether the company seems stable, profitable, and well-managed. Suppliers may rely on them indirectly when deciding how much credit to offer. Tax authorities rely on them to support tax reporting. Even potential buyers of a business will want to examine financial reports before agreeing to any price.

Inside the business, the reports shape decisions constantly. A retail store may decide whether to open another branch based on financial performance. A service business may revise its pricing after noticing that revenue is rising but profit is not. A startup may discover that it is surviving only because borrowed cash is keeping it afloat, not because operations are yet strong enough.

Financial reports also make communication easier. Instead of saying, "I think we're doing okay," a manager can say, "Revenue is up 12 percent, gross profit has improved, but cash from operations is under pressure because receivables are rising." That kind of language changes the quality of decision-making.

A business that ignores financial reports is often operating in a fog. Some survive for a while on energy, demand, or luck. But sooner or later, lack of visibility catches up with them. Costs creep up. Cash gets tight. Debt grows quietly. Opportunities are missed. Problems are noticed too late.

The reports do not solve every problem, but they help a business see the truth in time to act.

UNDERSTANDING FINANCIAL REPORTING PERIODS

Financial statements are always tied to a reporting period. This is easy to overlook, but it matters a great deal.

A business may operate continuously, but its financial results have to be measured in chunks of time. Those chunks could be a month, a quarter, or a year. The chosen period determines what gets included in the report and what belongs to a later one.

The income statement and cash flow statement cover a period of time. They answer questions like, "What happened during March?" or "What happened during the year ending December 31?" They track movement across time.

The balance sheet is different. It shows financial position at a specific date. It answers the question, "Where does the business stand right now?" If the date is December 31, the balance sheet is a snapshot of that exact moment.

This distinction matters because it changes how the reports are read.

An income statement for January through March tells a story of activity over three months. A balance sheet dated March 31 tells a story of position on that date alone.

Reporting periods are important for comparison. A business may compare one quarter to the previous quarter, or one year to the previous year, to see whether performance is improving or weakening. But those comparisons only make sense when the periods are understood clearly.

A seasonal business is a good example. A company that sells school supplies may have very strong results before a new school term and weaker results during quieter months. Looking at only one month without context could lead to the wrong conclusion. Reporting periods help place results in proper perspective.

They also matter for timing adjustments. A business must decide which revenues and expenses belong inside the reporting period and which belong outside it. That is why adjusting entries matter so much. They help make sure the statement for a given period truly reflects that period.

For example, if a business closes its books on June 30, then wages earned by employees up to June 30 should be recognized in that period, even if payment happens in July. The same logic applies to earned revenue not yet collected, prepaid expenses partly used up, and all the other timing issues that accounting tries to handle fairly.

Financial reporting periods also shape expectations. A monthly statement may be useful for close internal monitoring. A quarterly report may be useful for management reviews or investor updates. An annual report often supports tax reporting, external reviews, and long-term analysis.

One overlooked benefit of regular reporting periods is discipline. They force the business to stop, measure, and reflect. That rhythm matters. It prevents the business from drifting too long without checking its financial direction.

In that sense, reporting periods are not just about dates on paper. They are part of how a business stays aware of itself.

When people first encounter financial statements, they sometimes focus only on the numbers and forget the timing. But numbers without timing can be misleading. A strong figure may be less impressive if it took too long to achieve. A weak month may matter less if the business is highly seasonal. A cash squeeze may make more sense when looked at in the context of quarterly billing cycles.

That is why every financial statement should be read with one eye on the numbers and the other eye on the period being reported. Timing gives meaning to the figures. Without it, even accurate numbers can be misunderstood.

CHAPTER 12

THE INCOME STATEMENT

If someone asked, "Is this business actually making money?" the income statement is usually the first place to look.

It is one of the most talked-about financial reports because it gets straight to a question that matters to almost everyone connected to a business. Owners care about it. Managers care about it. lenders care about it. investors care about it. Even employees in leadership roles often care about it because it shows whether the business is producing enough income to support growth, stability, and better decisions.

The income statement tells the story of performance over a period of time. It shows what the business earned, what it spent to earn that money, and what remained after the dust settled. In plain terms, it answers a question every business has to face sooner or later: after all the work, sales, invoices, deliveries, salaries, supplies, and bills, what is left?

For beginners, the income statement can feel a bit formal at first. The layout looks serious. The labels sound technical. But the basic idea is familiar. It is really an organized version of something people ask in everyday life all the time: what came in, what went out, and what remained?

A market trader might not call it an income statement, but when they mentally compare today's sales to the money spent on stock, transport, and stall fees, they are already thinking in that direction. A freelancer comparing client payments to software costs, internet bills, and travel costs is doing something similar. The income statement simply gives that thinking a more structured form.

Once you understand how it works, it becomes one of the clearest windows into the health of a business.

WHAT THE INCOME STATEMENT SHOWS

The income statement shows the financial performance of a business over a specific period. That period could be a month, a quarter, or a year. Unlike the balance sheet, which is a snapshot taken at one moment, the income statement is more like a short film. It captures movement across time.

It focuses on three broad ideas:

- revenue
- expenses
- profit or loss

Revenue is the money earned from the business's main activities. Expenses are the costs incurred in generating that revenue. Profit is what remains after expenses are subtracted from revenue. If expenses are greater than revenue, the result is a loss.

That structure sounds simple, and in one sense it is. But the power of the income statement lies in how clearly it separates business performance from guesswork.

Many businesses feel busy. Phones ring. orders come in. Customers show interest. Staff stay occupied. But activity and profitability are not the same thing. A business can look successful on the surface while quietly losing money because its costs are too high, its pricing is too low, or its operations are poorly controlled.

The income statement helps cut through appearances.

Suppose a small catering business completes ten events in a month and brings in what seems like good money.

Without an income statement, the owner may assume the month went well. But once the numbers are laid out, the picture might be different. Perhaps food costs rose sharply. Maybe transport costs were higher than usual. Maybe casual staff wages increased because of last-minute bookings. Once those costs are included, profit may be far smaller than expected.

That is why the income statement matters. It shows whether the business is truly earning enough after covering the cost of doing business.

It also helps identify patterns. A business might notice that revenue is growing while profit stays flat. That can signal rising costs or weak pricing. Another business may see that even modest revenue leads to healthy profit because costs are tightly controlled. Both insights matter.

An income statement also helps with timing. It gathers revenue and expenses that belong to the same period, which makes the result more meaningful. If prepared properly, it tells a fair story about what that month or year actually produced.

A person reading the income statement is usually trying to understand performance, not just transactions. They want to know whether the business is moving in the right direction.

That is why this report tends to get so much attention. It gives shape to a very practical question: is the business creating value, or is it burning effort without enough return?

REVENUE AND COST OF GOODS SOLD

One of the first important sections on many income statements is the relationship between **revenue** and **cost of goods sold**.

Revenue is the amount earned from selling goods or services. It is the top line of the income statement, and for that reason, people sometimes refer to revenue growth as "growing the top line." Revenue matters because it reflects demand. It shows that customers are willing to pay for what the business offers.

But revenue alone does not say enough.

A business might generate strong sales and still struggle badly if the direct cost of producing or acquiring what it sells is too high. That is where cost of goods sold comes in.

Cost of goods sold, often shortened to COGS, refers to the direct cost tied to the goods or services sold during the period. For a retail store, this usually means the cost of purchasing the products that were later sold to customers. For a manufacturer, it includes materials and direct production costs. For a bakery, it may include flour, sugar, butter, packaging, and other ingredients directly used in making items sold. For some service businesses, this line may be smaller or handled differently, but the principle remains the same: it captures the direct cost connected to what was earned.

The difference between revenue and cost of goods sold is called **gross profit**.

That figure matters because it shows how much money is left after covering the most direct costs of what was sold. It does not yet account for rent, salaries, advertising, and other operating expenses, but it does tell you whether the core offering has enough financial strength to support the rest of the business.

Take a simple example.

A small clothing shop earns $20,000 in sales during a month. The clothes sold during that month cost the business $11,000 to purchase from suppliers.

That means:

Revenue = $20,000
Cost of Goods Sold = $11,000
Gross Profit = $9,000

That $9,000 is what remains to cover all the other costs of running the business.

Now consider what this reveals. If the shop had made $20,000 in sales but the cost of the goods sold was $18,500, the gross profit would be much smaller. That would leave far less room for rent, salaries, utilities, and profit. So even before looking at the rest of the income statement, the relationship between revenue and cost of goods sold already tells you something important about the business.

This is one reason gross profit is watched so closely. It reflects whether the business is buying, producing, or pricing well enough at the core level.

Let us bring this into a more relatable setting.

Imagine a small cake business. During a busy month, it sells custom cakes and earns $5,000 in revenue. The ingredients, cake boards, decorations, and packaging directly used for those cakes cost $2,000.

That leaves a gross profit of $3,000.

That sounds healthy at first glance, but whether the month ends well depends on what happens next. The business still needs to pay delivery costs, electricity, advertising, rent, and perhaps assistant wages. Still, gross profit is encouraging because it shows the cakes themselves are generating financial room.

If gross profit is weak, the business may need to look at pricing, supplier costs, waste, production efficiency, or product mix. Sometimes a business has no revenue problem at all. It has a gross margin problem.

So when reading the income statement, it helps not to jump straight from revenue to final profit. The space in between contains useful clues. Revenue says the business sold. Cost of goods sold says what it took directly to make those sales happen. Gross profit shows what is left before the rest of the business enters the picture.

OPERATING EXPENSES EXPLAINED

Once direct costs are covered, the business still has the everyday cost of staying alive.

These are known as **operating expenses.** They are the regular costs of running the business that are not directly tied to producing a specific product or service unit.

If cost of goods sold reflects the cost of the item itself, operating expenses reflect the cost of running the environment around that item.

Common operating expenses include:

- rent
- salaries and wages
- utilities
- office supplies
- advertising
- internet and phone bills
- insurance
- software subscriptions
- transportation
- repairs and maintenance
- professional fees

These costs may not attach neatly to one sale, but without them, the business could not function properly.

Imagine a salon. The shampoos, hair dye, and styling products used directly for clients may be treated as direct service costs or cost of sales, depending on the setup. But the rent for the salon space, the receptionist's pay, the electricity bill, the booking software subscription, the cleaning costs, and the marketing flyer expenses are operating expenses.

They are real costs. They matter deeply. They are simply one step removed from the direct making of the sale.

This distinction is important because businesses often underestimate the impact of operating expenses. A product may seem profitable when looking only at sales and direct costs, but once operating expenses are included, the picture can change dramatically.

Suppose a small online business sells home décor items. Sales are solid. Gross profit looks respectable. But then come the monthly advertising costs, warehouse rent, packaging admin costs, website fees, staff salaries, and customer service costs. Suddenly, final profit shrinks. The business is not necessarily failing, but it is carrying more overhead than the owner may have realized.

Operating expenses help answer a more mature business question: not just "Can we sell this profitably?" but "Can we run the whole business sustainably?"

That is a bigger question, and it matters just as much.

Some operating expenses are fairly fixed, meaning they do not change much from month to month. Rent is a good example. Some are more flexible or variable, such as advertising or fuel. Some grow as the business expands. Others may remain stable for a while and then jump when the business moves to a larger space or hires more staff.

This is why owners and managers often study operating expenses carefully. They want to know whether costs are being controlled, whether spending is producing enough value, and whether the business structure is becoming too expensive.

A useful way to think about operating expenses is that they represent the cost of maintaining the business engine while it runs. They may not create revenue directly one unit at a time, but they make revenue possible.

There is also an emotional side to this. Operating expenses are often where small businesses feel pressure most sharply. It is one thing to buy stock when sales are moving. It is another thing to pay rent during a slow month, cover salaries when clients delay payment, or keep software subscriptions active even when cash is tight. That is why understanding operating expenses is not just a reporting exercise. It is part of running a business with open eyes.

When income statements are read carefully, operating expenses often reveal where business discipline is strongest or weakest. They show how much it costs to support the structure of the business and whether that structure makes sense given current revenue levels.

CALCULATING PROFIT AND NET INCOME

After revenue is listed, direct costs are subtracted, and operating expenses are taken into account, the income statement moves toward one of its most watched figures: **profit**.

Profit is the financial reward for running the business successfully enough to earn more than it spends. It is not the only measure that matters, but it is certainly one of the most important.

There are usually a few stages on the way to final profit.

First comes **gross profit**, which is revenue minus cost of goods sold.

Then, after operating expenses are subtracted, the business arrives at **operating profit** or a similar intermediate figure, depending on the reporting format.

After that, other items may be considered, such as interest expense, taxes, or other gains and losses. What remains at the end is often called **net income**, **net profit**, or simply the bottom line.

Net income is the amount left after all relevant expenses have been deducted from revenue.

This is the number many people focus on because it captures the overall result of the period. It answers the question: after covering everything, what did the business actually keep?

Let us use a simple example.

A small printing business has the following figures for the month:

Revenue: $12,000
Cost of Goods Sold: $4,500
Gross Profit: $7,500

Operating expenses:

- Rent: $1,500
- Salaries: $2,200
- Utilities: $300
- Advertising: $400
- Internet and software: $200

Total operating expenses: $4,600

Operating profit: $2,900

Then suppose the business also pays:

- Loan interest: $200

Now profit before tax becomes $2,700

If taxes are ignored for simplicity at this stage, net income is $2,700.

That $2,700 is the final earnings result for the month.

Now let us slow down and notice something important. The business generated $12,000 in revenue, but only $2,700 remained as net income. That does not mean the business performed poorly. It means the full income statement tells a richer story than sales alone ever could.

This is why beginners often have a breakthrough moment when they start reading income statements properly. They realize that strong sales do not automatically mean strong profit. Profit depends on what it cost to generate and support those sales.

Net income also matters because it flows into the broader financial picture. Profit increases the business's equity if retained in the business. Losses reduce it. So net income is not just an ending number on one report. It influences the business's overall financial position.

There is another practical point worth noting. Profit is not the same thing as cash in hand. A business can report net income and still feel cash pressure if customers have not paid, inventory was purchased heavily, or loan repayments are draining the bank account. That is why the income statement must eventually be read alongside the balance sheet and cash flow statement.

Still, net income remains central because it measures whether the business's activities, taken as a whole, are financially worthwhile.

A business owner might tolerate a short-term loss during early growth. Another may accept lower profit in exchange for expansion. But over time, most businesses need some level of healthy net income to survive, invest, and reward the effort involved.

EXAMPLE OF A SIMPLE INCOME STATEMENT

It often helps to see everything come together in a clean example.

Imagine a small business called **Bright Path Stationery**, which sells notebooks, pens, and office supplies from a modest retail shop and a small online page.

For the month of June, the business reports the following:

- Sales revenue: $18,000
- Cost of inventory sold: $9,500
- Rent: $2,000
- Staff wages: $2,800
- Utilities: $350

- Advertising: $450
- Internet and software: $200
- Delivery and transport: $300
- Loan interest: $150

A simple income statement might look like this:

Bright Path Stationery
Income Statement
For the Month Ended June 30

Sales Revenue $18,000
Cost of Goods Sold .... (9,500)
Gross Profit $8,500

Operating Expenses:
Rent Expense $2,000
Wages Expense 2,800
Utilities Expense 350
Advertising Expense 450
Internet and Software Expense 200
Delivery and Transport Expense 300

Total Operating Expenses .... (6,100)
Operating Profit $2,400

Interest Expense .... (150)
Net Income $2,250

Now let us read it like a real person rather than just staring at the layout.

The business brought in $18,000 in sales. The goods sold cost $9,500, leaving $8,500 in gross profit. That is a useful sign because it shows the products themselves are generating room to support the business.

Then come the operating expenses. Together, they total $6,100. These are the costs of keeping the shop running: people, space, electricity, visibility, and systems.

After those costs, the business is left with $2,400 in operating profit. Then interest expense reduces the final result slightly, leaving net income of $2,250.

What does that tell us?

It tells us the business was profitable for the month. It also tells us that wages and rent are major cost areas, which is common in retail. It shows that the business is not keeping a huge share of sales as net income, but it is still earning a positive result.

A thoughtful owner might ask:

- Can we improve our gross margin?

- Are wages at the right level for our current sales?
- Is advertising bringing enough return?
- Could delivery costs be managed better?
- Are we comfortable with this profit level, or do we need to improve it?

That is the real value of the income statement. It does not merely present numbers. It invites better questions.

Let us take one more quick example from a service business to show how the pattern can differ slightly.

Imagine **Clear Voice Media**, a freelance content and editing business.

For the month:

- Service revenue: $6,500
- Direct contractor support: $1,000
- Internet and software: $250
- Marketing: $300
- Home office expenses: $400
- Travel: $150

A simple income statement could be:

Service Revenue		$6,500
Direct Project Costs		(1,000)
Gross Profit	$5,500	

Operating Expenses:		
Internet and Software		250
Marketing Expense		300
Home Office Expense		400
Travel Expense	150	

Total Operating Expenses		(1,100)
Net Income	$4,400	

This business has a very different cost structure. It has lower overhead and fewer direct costs, so a larger portion of revenue remains as profit. That does not automatically make it a better business, but it does show how income statements reflect the economic reality of different business models.

A retail shop, a bakery, a printing company, a coaching service, and a freelance designer may all use income statements, but the patterns inside them will not look exactly the same. That is part of what makes the report so useful. It adapts to the shape of the business while still following the same underlying logic.

Once you can read an income statement comfortably, you begin to see more than numbers. You start seeing pressure points, strengths, waste, discipline, opportunity, and the basic financial truth of how a business is performing over time.

CHAPTER 13

THE BALANCE SHEET

If the income statement tells the story of how a business performed over time, the balance sheet answers a different question: **Where does the business stand right now?**

It is often described as a snapshot of the business at a specific moment. While the income statement stretches across a period of time, the balance sheet freezes everything at a particular date and shows the financial position at that point.

This report lists three essential elements:

- what the business owns
- what the business owes
- what belongs to the owner after debts are considered

These three elements correspond to the familiar accounting equation:

Assets = Liabilities + Equity

That simple relationship lies at the heart of the balance sheet. Everything the business owns must have come from somewhere. It may have been funded by borrowing money, or by investment and profit belonging to the owner. The balance sheet shows both sides of that story at once.

For someone new to accounting, the balance sheet can feel like a structured inventory of financial reality. It gathers the value of assets, the obligations owed to others, and the owner's stake in the business into one place. When viewed together, these elements reveal whether a business is financially stable, stretched, or somewhere in between.

A balance sheet also helps answer practical questions.

Does the business have enough assets to cover its debts?
How much of the business is financed by borrowing?
Is the owner building financial value over time?
Are resources being used productively?

These questions matter whether the business is small or large. A freelancer working from home, a retail shop on a busy street, and a growing company with dozens of employees all rely on the same basic structure to understand their financial position.

Once the balance sheet becomes familiar, it starts to feel less like a formal accounting document and more like a map of the business's financial landscape.

WHAT THE BALANCE SHEET REVEALS

The balance sheet reveals the financial position of a business at a specific date.

Think of it as taking a photograph of the business's finances at the end of the month or year. The photograph captures everything the business currently owns and everything it currently owes. The difference between the two represents the owner's claim on the business.

Unlike the income statement, which focuses on activity, the balance sheet focuses on **position**.

To understand its value, imagine a small café at the end of the month. The café may have:

- cash in the bank
- coffee machines and kitchen equipment
- furniture and tables
- ingredients in storage
- unpaid invoices from catering clients

These are assets.

At the same time, the café may owe:

- money to suppliers
- rent to the landlord
- wages to employees
- loan payments to the bank

These are liabilities.

What remains after subtracting liabilities from assets belongs to the owner. That remaining portion is equity.

Looking at the balance sheet allows someone to see the overall structure of the business. It shows how resources are arranged and how they are financed.

For example, a business might own a large amount of equipment but also carry significant loans used to purchase that equipment. Another business might own fewer assets but have little or no debt. The balance sheet makes these differences visible.

It also helps assess financial stability. If a business has strong assets but very little cash, it might struggle with day-to-day expenses. If liabilities are growing faster than assets, the business could be moving toward financial pressure.

Another insight the balance sheet provides is how much of the business belongs to the owner through accumulated profits and investments. Over time, healthy businesses tend to build equity. That equity represents value created through successful operations.

So the balance sheet does more than simply list numbers. It shows the financial structure supporting the entire business.

CURRENT VS. NON-CURRENT ASSETS

Assets represent resources owned or controlled by the business that have economic value. These resources help the business operate, generate revenue, and support long-term growth.

Assets are usually divided into two categories:

- current assets
- non-current assets

This distinction helps readers understand how quickly those assets can be converted into cash or used in normal business operations.

Current Assets

Current assets are resources that are expected to be used, sold, or converted into cash within one year or within the normal operating cycle of the business.

Common current assets include:

- cash
- accounts receivable
- inventory
- short-term investments
- prepaid expenses

Cash is the most straightforward asset. It includes money in bank accounts or readily available funds that the business can use immediately.

Accounts receivable represent money owed by customers who have received goods or services but have not yet paid. For example, a consulting firm may complete a project and send an invoice with payment due in thirty days. That unpaid amount becomes an asset until the customer pays.

Inventory is the stock of goods held for sale. A clothing shop may have shirts, jackets, and accessories waiting to be sold. A bakery may have ingredients and finished products. Until these items are sold, they remain part of the business's assets.

Prepaid expenses are payments made in advance for services the business will use later. Insurance is a common example. If a business pays a year's insurance premium upfront, the unused portion is treated as an asset until the coverage period passes.

Current assets matter because they support the day-to-day functioning of the business. They represent resources that will soon turn into revenue or be used to keep operations running.

Non-Current Assets

Non-current assets, sometimes called long-term assets, are resources that provide value over a longer period of time. They are not expected to be converted into cash or fully used within a year.

Examples include:

- buildings
- machinery
- vehicles
- furniture
- computers

- land

These assets are often essential for running the business but are not intended to be sold quickly.

Consider a delivery company that owns several vans. Those vans help generate revenue every day, but they are not sold as part of the company's normal operations. Instead, they support the business over several years.

Similarly, a manufacturing business may rely on heavy machinery that produces goods for a long time. These machines represent a significant investment, and their value is gradually allocated over time through depreciation.

Separating current and non-current assets helps readers understand liquidity. Liquidity refers to how easily a business can access cash or resources to meet short-term obligations.

A business with strong current assets relative to its short-term liabilities is usually in a better position to manage everyday expenses. On the other hand, a business whose assets are mostly tied up in long-term equipment might face cash flow pressure if bills come due quickly.

This classification helps financial statements communicate more than just total value. It shows how flexible the business's resources are.

UNDERSTANDING LIABILITIES

While assets represent what a business owns, liabilities represent what it owes.

Liabilities are obligations the business must eventually settle, usually by paying cash, delivering goods, or providing services. These obligations often arise from borrowing money, purchasing supplies on credit, or incurring expenses that will be paid later.

Just like assets, liabilities are commonly divided into two groups:

- current liabilities
- long-term liabilities

Current Liabilities

Current liabilities are obligations expected to be settled within one year.

Examples include:

- accounts payable

- wages payable
- short-term loans
- taxes payable
- utilities payable

Accounts payable represent amounts owed to suppliers. If a restaurant purchases ingredients on credit from a food supplier, the unpaid amount appears as accounts payable until payment is made.

Wages payable arise when employees have earned wages that have not yet been paid. For instance, if staff work during the final days of the month but payroll occurs next month, the business still owes those wages.

Taxes payable represent obligations to government authorities. These might include payroll taxes, sales taxes, or income taxes depending on the business structure.

Current liabilities are closely watched because they represent obligations that must be handled soon. A business needs sufficient current assets or cash flow to meet these responsibilities.

Long-Term Liabilities

Long-term liabilities are obligations that extend beyond one year.

Common examples include:

- bank loans
- mortgages
- long-term lease obligations

A business might take out a loan to purchase equipment, renovate a building, or expand operations. These loans are typically repaid over several years.

Long-term liabilities are not necessarily negative. In many cases, borrowing allows a business to invest in growth or acquire assets that would otherwise be unaffordable.

However, too much debt can create financial strain. If loan payments become difficult to manage, the business may struggle with cash flow and financial stability.

This is why lenders and investors pay close attention to the balance between assets and liabilities. They want to understand how much of the business's resources are financed through borrowing and whether those obligations are manageable.

Liabilities tell part of the story of how the business was built. Some resources may come from owner investment, while others may come from borrowed funds.

Understanding that balance is essential for evaluating financial health.

OWNER'S EQUITY EXPLAINED

Owner's equity represents the owner's financial interest in the business. It is the portion of assets that remains after all liabilities have been deducted.

In simple terms, equity shows what truly belongs to the owner.

It can grow or shrink over time depending on several factors.

Equity increases when:

- the owner invests money in the business
- the business earns profit and retains it

Equity decreases when:

- the business experiences losses
- the owner withdraws money for personal use

Suppose an entrepreneur starts a small design studio by investing $10,000 of personal savings. That investment becomes part of the business's equity.

If the studio later earns $5,000 in profit and the owner leaves the money in the business, equity increases. The business now holds more value belonging to the owner.

However, if the owner withdraws $2,000 for personal expenses, equity decreases because part of the business's resources have been taken out.

Over time, successful businesses often build equity through accumulated profits. That growing equity reflects the value created through operations.

Equity can include several accounts depending on the business structure. In a small sole proprietorship, it may simply appear as owner's capital and owner's withdrawals. In larger companies, it may include retained earnings and other equity components.

Regardless of structure, equity connects the income statement to the balance sheet. When a business earns profit, that profit ultimately increases the owner's stake in the business.

Equity therefore represents both past investment and the accumulated results of running the business over time.

For many entrepreneurs, growing equity is one of the long-term goals of operating a business. It represents financial progress and the building of lasting value.

EXAMPLE OF A BALANCE SHEET

Seeing the balance sheet in action helps bring these ideas together.

Imagine a small business called **Green Valley Landscaping** at the end of the year. The company provides garden maintenance and landscaping services.

The business owns several assets:

- cash in the bank
- equipment such as lawnmowers and tools
- a work vehicle
- unpaid invoices from customers

It also has some obligations:

- money owed to suppliers
- a small equipment loan

A simplified balance sheet might look like this:

Green Valley Landscaping
Balance Sheet
December 31

Assets
Cash $8,500
Accounts Receivable 2,200
Equipment 7,000
Vehicle 12,000

Total Assets $29,700

Liabilities
Accounts Payable $2,000
Equipment Loan 5,000

Total Liabilities $7,000

Owner's Equity
Owner's Capital $22,700

Total Liabilities and Equity $29,700

Notice how both sides of the balance sheet match. The total value of assets equals the total of liabilities plus equity. This balance reflects the accounting equation in action.

Looking at the numbers reveals several insights.

The business owns valuable equipment and a vehicle that support its operations. It also has some outstanding invoices from customers, which means additional cash should arrive soon.

Its liabilities are relatively modest compared with its assets. This suggests the company is not heavily dependent on borrowing.

The owner's equity is the largest portion of the balance sheet, which often indicates that the business has been built largely through investment and accumulated profits rather than heavy debt.

Someone analyzing this balance sheet might conclude that the business has a solid financial foundation. It owns useful resources, carries manageable obligations, and retains significant owner value.

That is the real strength of the balance sheet. It organizes financial information into a structure that allows readers to quickly understand the financial position of the business.

When combined with the income statement and cash flow statement, it becomes part of a larger picture that explains not only how the business performed, but also how it is positioned for the future.

CHAPTER 14

THE CASH FLOW STATEMENT

A business can report strong sales, healthy profit, and still struggle to pay its bills. That situation surprises many people the first time they encounter it, but it happens more often than expected. The reason is simple: **profit and cash are not the same thing**.

The income statement measures performance. The balance sheet shows financial position. But neither of them alone explains exactly how cash moved through the business. That missing piece is where the cash flow statement comes in.

The cash flow statement tracks the movement of money in and out of the business during a specific period. It answers questions that many business owners find themselves asking in practical situations:

Why does the business show a profit but the bank balance feels tight?
Where did the extra cash come from this month?
Did we generate cash from operations, or did we borrow it?

How much cash did we spend on equipment or expansion?

Cash is the fuel that keeps the business engine running. A profitable company that runs out of cash can quickly face serious trouble. Employees still expect wages. Suppliers still expect payment. Rent still comes due. The business might have valuable assets and strong sales, but without available cash, operations can grind to a halt.

This is why experienced business owners often say something that sounds surprising at first: **profit is important, but cash flow is survival**.

The cash flow statement provides a clear explanation of how money actually moved during a reporting period. It organizes these movements into three major categories:

- operating activities
- investing activities
- financing activities

Together, these sections tell the story of how the business generated cash, how it used that cash, and whether it ended the period stronger or weaker financially.

Once this report becomes familiar, it adds an entirely new layer of understanding to financial statements. Instead of simply seeing profits and assets, you begin to see the real financial rhythm of the business.

WHY CASH FLOW MATTERS

Cash flow matters because it determines whether a business can function smoothly in everyday operations.

Imagine a small construction company that completes several large projects during the year. The company records strong revenue and profit because the projects were successful. However, most clients pay only after long billing cycles. Meanwhile, the company must pay workers weekly and purchase materials upfront.

On paper, the business looks profitable. In reality, it may struggle with cash shortages while waiting for payments to arrive.

This situation illustrates why understanding cash flow is so important.

Profit measures whether the business earned more than it spent. Cash flow measures whether money actually moved in time to support operations. A business needs both.

There are several reasons cash flow plays such a central role in financial health.

First, cash flow keeps operations running. Wages, rent, utilities, supplies, and loan payments usually require cash, not accounting profit.

Second, cash flow determines whether a business can grow. Expansion often requires purchasing equipment, hiring employees, investing in marketing, or opening new locations. Without available cash or access to financing, these opportunities may remain out of reach.

Third, cash flow influences financial stability. A company with steady positive cash flow has flexibility. It can handle unexpected expenses, invest in improvements, and survive short-term challenges. A company with weak cash flow may find itself constantly reacting to financial pressure.

Fourth, cash flow helps identify hidden problems. If a business shows healthy profit but negative cash flow, something may be wrong. Perhaps customers are taking too long to pay. Maybe inventory purchases are too high. Maybe operating costs are rising faster than revenue.

The cash flow statement reveals these patterns in a way that the income statement alone cannot.

Think of cash flow like the bloodstream of a business. Revenue and profit may describe the body's strength, but cash flow shows whether energy is actually circulating where it needs to go.

A company can survive temporary profit dips if cash reserves are strong. But a company that runs out of cash rarely has time to fix deeper problems.

For that reason, many experienced managers check cash flow reports just as closely as profit figures.

OPERATING ACTIVITIES

Operating activities represent the cash generated or used by the core business operations. These activities relate to the everyday work of producing goods, delivering services, and managing routine expenses.

In simple terms, operating cash flow answers the question: **Did the business generate cash from its normal activities?**

Typical operating activities include:

- cash received from customers
- cash paid to suppliers
- wages paid to employees
- payments for utilities, rent, and other operating expenses
- taxes paid to government authorities

This section of the cash flow statement often begins with net income and then adjusts that figure to reflect actual cash movement.

Why are adjustments needed?

Because the income statement includes items that affect profit but not immediate cash flow. For example, revenue might be recorded before customers pay, creating accounts receivable. Similarly, expenses may appear on the income statement before the cash leaves the business.

Operating cash flow adjusts for these timing differences.

Consider a small consulting firm that earned $10,000 in revenue during the month but collected only $7,000 from clients. The remaining $3,000 sits in accounts receivable.

The income statement reports the full $10,000 because the services were delivered. But the cash flow statement focuses on the $7,000 actually received during the period.

The same logic applies to expenses. Suppose the firm incurred $1,200 in utility costs but paid only $900 before the end of the month. The unpaid portion remains as a liability.

Operating cash flow highlights the money that actually moved.

A business with strong operating cash flow is generally in a healthy position. It means the business's main activities are generating enough cash to support operations.

When operating cash flow is consistently negative, it can signal deeper issues. The business may rely on loans or outside investment to stay afloat. That may be manageable for a short period, but long-term sustainability usually requires positive operating cash flow.

One helpful way to think about operating activities is to imagine the daily heartbeat of the business. These are the regular financial movements that occur as the company delivers value to customers and pays the costs of doing so.

When that heartbeat is steady, the business tends to feel stable.

INVESTING ACTIVITIES

While operating activities focus on daily operations, investing activities focus on **long-term growth and asset management**.

Investing activities involve the purchase or sale of long-term assets used by the business. These assets support operations over several years rather than being consumed immediately.

Examples include:

- purchasing equipment
- buying vehicles
- acquiring buildings or land
- investing in technology systems
- selling long-term assets no longer needed

These transactions may not happen every day, but they often involve significant amounts of money.

Imagine a small delivery company that decides to expand its fleet by purchasing two additional vans. The purchase represents an investing activity because the vehicles are long-term assets that will support the business over time.

In the cash flow statement, this purchase appears as a cash outflow under investing activities.

Similarly, if the company later sells an old vehicle that is no longer needed, the cash received from that sale would appear as an inflow in the investing section.

Investing activities often reflect strategic decisions about the future of the business.

A company that invests heavily in equipment or technology may be preparing for expansion. A company selling major assets may be restructuring or reducing operations.

These activities do not necessarily indicate immediate profit or loss. Instead, they show how the business is allocating resources for long-term development.

For example, a manufacturing company might spend a large amount of cash purchasing new machinery. That investment reduces cash in the short term, but it could increase production capacity and future revenue.

In that sense, investing activities tell part of the story of how the business is positioning itself for tomorrow.

FINANCING ACTIVITIES

Financing activities involve transactions that affect how the business is funded.

Every business must obtain financial resources in order to operate. These resources may come from owners, investors, or lenders. Financing activities show how money flows between the business and those providers of capital.

Common financing activities include:

- borrowing money from banks
- repaying loans
- receiving investments from owners or shareholders
- paying dividends or owner withdrawals

These transactions influence the structure of the balance sheet by affecting liabilities and equity.

For instance, suppose a small manufacturing company takes out a $50,000 bank loan to purchase new equipment. The loan provides cash to the business, so it appears as an inflow in the financing section of the cash flow statement.

Later, when the company repays part of that loan, the payment appears as an outflow under financing activities.

Owner contributions and withdrawals are also included in this section. When an owner injects personal funds into the business, the company receives cash, which strengthens its financial position. When the owner withdraws money, the opposite occurs.

Financing activities reveal how dependent the business is on external funding.

A company that frequently borrows money may be using debt to support growth. That approach can be effective if managed carefully. However, excessive borrowing can create financial pressure if loan repayments become difficult to maintain.

On the other hand, a business that relies mainly on operating cash flow may have greater financial independence.

The financing section helps readers understand the broader financial strategy behind the numbers.

It answers questions such as:

Is the business funding its growth through profits or borrowing?
Is the company paying back debt or accumulating more?
Are owners investing additional capital or withdrawing funds?

These insights are important for anyone evaluating the long-term stability of a business.

EXAMPLE OF A CASH FLOW STATEMENT

Seeing a simplified example helps bring all three sections together.

Imagine a small company called **Riverstone Outdoor Gear**, which sells camping equipment and hiking accessories.

At the start of the month, the business had $5,000 in cash.

During the month, several financial activities occurred:

- Customers paid $18,000 for products

- The company paid $10,500 to suppliers and employees
- A new delivery vehicle was purchased for $6,000
- The owner invested an additional $3,000 into the business

The cash flow statement might look like this:

Riverstone Outdoor Gear
Cash Flow Statement
For the Month Ended March 31

Operating Activities
Cash received from customers $18,000
Cash paid to suppliers and employees ..... (10,500)

Net Cash from Operating Activities $7,500

Investing Activities
Purchase of delivery vehicle .... (6,000)

Net Cash Used in Investing Activities ...... (6,000)

Financing Activities
Owner investment 3,000

Net Cash from Financing Activities 3,000

Net Increase in Cash $4,500

Beginning Cash Balance 5,000

Ending Cash Balance $9,500

Looking at this statement reveals several insights.

The business generated $7,500 in cash from its core operations, which is a positive sign. It spent $6,000 on a new vehicle, indicating investment in future operations. The owner also contributed additional capital, increasing available resources.

At the end of the month, the company's cash balance grew from $5,000 to $9,500.

This single report shows how operating success, strategic investment, and owner financing combined to strengthen the company's cash position.

Without the cash flow statement, it might be difficult to see how those movements interacted.

The income statement might show profit, and the balance sheet might show assets and liabilities. But the cash flow statement explains the journey of money through the business.

It reveals where cash originated, how it was used, and whether the business finished the period financially stronger than when it began.

Understanding that journey is one of the most valuable skills a business owner can develop.

CHAPTER 15

CONNECTING THE FINANCIAL STATEMENTS

When people first encounter financial statements, they often study them one at a time. The income statement shows profit. The balance sheet shows assets and liabilities. The cash flow statement shows the movement of money. Each report seems clear enough on its own.

The real insight comes when these reports are read **together**.

Financial statements are not separate documents that happen to share similar numbers. They are tightly connected pieces of the same financial system. The activity recorded in one report influences the others. A change in profit affects equity. Cash collected from customers changes both the cash flow statement and the balance sheet. A loan affects financing cash flow while also increasing liabilities.

Once this connection becomes clear, financial reports start to feel less like isolated tables and more like parts of a single conversation about the business.

Think of a business like a living system. Sales generate revenue. Revenue creates profit. Profit increases equity. Cash flows in and out to support operations and investments. The balance sheet reflects the accumulated results of these activities. Each statement captures a different view of that process.

Understanding how these reports interact transforms financial reading from simple observation into meaningful interpretation.

Instead of asking only "What does this report say?" you begin asking "How does this report relate to the others?"

That shift turns financial statements into a powerful tool for understanding how a business truly operates.

HOW THE INCOME STATEMENT AFFECTS THE BALANCE SHEET

One of the most important connections in financial accounting lies between the income statement and the balance sheet.

The income statement measures performance over a period of time. It calculates profit by subtracting expenses from revenue. But that profit does not simply disappear when the period ends. It becomes part of the business's accumulated value.

This is where the balance sheet comes in.

The balance sheet contains an equity section that represents the owner's financial interest in the business. When a business earns profit and keeps that profit within the company rather than distributing it, equity increases.

Imagine a small consulting business that begins the year with $30,000 in owner's equity. Over the year, the company earns $8,000 in net income. If the owner does not withdraw that money, the equity on the balance sheet increases to $38,000.

The income statement recorded the profit. The balance sheet shows where that profit ended up.

Losses work the same way in the opposite direction. If expenses exceed revenue, the resulting loss reduces equity. The business has effectively consumed some of the value previously accumulated.

This connection between profit and equity reflects a simple idea: business results eventually change the financial position of the company.

Revenue and expenses themselves do not appear permanently on the balance sheet. They belong to the income statement because they describe activity during a period. Once that activity is summarized into profit or loss, the result flows into equity on the balance sheet.

There are other links as well.

Suppose a business earns revenue but has not yet received payment from customers. The income statement still records the revenue because the service or product has been delivered. Meanwhile, the balance sheet shows an asset called accounts receivable, representing the money owed by those customers.

Expenses can have a similar connection. If the business receives a service but has not yet paid for it, the expense appears on the income statement while a liability appears on the balance sheet.

These interactions remind us that the income statement and balance sheet are two views of the same underlying transactions. One focuses on performance, while the other captures position.

Reading them together reveals how financial results shape the structure of the business over time.

HOW CASH FLOW REFLECTS BUSINESS ACTIVITY

The cash flow statement provides another crucial connection among financial reports.

While the income statement records revenue and expenses based on when they are earned or incurred, the cash flow statement focuses on when cash actually moves.

This difference explains why profit and cash do not always match perfectly.

Imagine a design studio that completes several projects in one month and sends invoices to clients. The income statement records revenue immediately because the work has been delivered. However, if clients take thirty days to pay, the cash has not yet arrived.

The balance sheet shows accounts receivable representing the money owed by clients. The cash flow statement, on the other hand, shows that cash has not yet been collected from those sales.

Eventually, when the client pays the invoice, the cash flow statement records an inflow of cash. The balance sheet reduces accounts receivable and increases cash.

Through this process, the cash flow statement acts as a bridge between profit and cash movement.

Operating activities in the cash flow statement relate closely to items in the income statement. They adjust profit to reflect actual cash movement by considering changes in working capital accounts such as receivables, inventory, and payables.

Investing activities connect with the balance sheet by reflecting purchases or sales of long-term assets. When a business buys equipment, cash decreases while the equipment account on the balance sheet increases.

Financing activities also connect with the balance sheet by showing how borrowing, loan repayments, and owner investments affect liabilities and equity.

Taken together, the cash flow statement explains how the business's activities translated into real money moving through the organization.

Without it, a reader might see profit but remain unsure how that profit influenced the company's liquidity.

UNDERSTANDING THE FINANCIAL STORY OF A BUSINESS

When financial statements are viewed together, they begin to tell a story.

The income statement describes what the business accomplished during the period. It shows how much revenue was generated and how effectively costs were managed.

The balance sheet reveals the accumulated results of those activities. It shows what resources the business now controls and how those resources are financed.

The cash flow statement explains how money moved while those events unfolded.

Reading the reports together allows a deeper understanding of the business.

Consider a retail store that reports rising revenue on the income statement. That seems promising. But if the balance sheet shows growing inventory levels and the cash flow statement reveals large cash outflows for stock purchases, the store may be investing heavily in inventory to support those sales.

Now imagine another scenario.

A company shows strong profit on the income statement, but the cash flow statement shows negative operating cash flow. The balance sheet reveals large increases in accounts receivable. This suggests that customers are taking longer to pay, which could create liquidity pressure even though the business appears profitable.

A third example might involve a business that recently purchased new equipment. The cash flow statement shows a large investing outflow. The balance sheet shows increased assets and possibly new loan liabilities. Meanwhile, the income statement might not yet show significant benefits from that investment.

In each of these situations, the financial statements combine to tell a broader story about the business.

Revenue growth may signal demand. Cash flow may reveal operational discipline. The balance sheet may show whether growth is financed by profit, borrowing, or new investment.

These patterns become clearer once the statements are read together rather than separately.

WHY THESE STATEMENTS MUST ALIGN

Because financial statements are connected, consistency between them is essential.

If the numbers in one report do not align with the others, it signals that something may be wrong with the accounting records.

For example, profit reported on the income statement should eventually influence equity on the balance sheet. If the equity balance never reflects accumulated profits, the records may be incomplete.

Similarly, changes in cash reported on the cash flow statement should match the change in the cash balance shown on the balance sheet.

If the cash flow statement reports an increase in cash of $4,000 during the period, the balance sheet should show that the ending cash balance increased by that same amount.

These relationships help accountants verify accuracy.

Financial statements are built from the same underlying data. When they align properly, it confirms that transactions were recorded correctly and that the accounting equation remains balanced.

Alignment also strengthens confidence in financial reporting. Investors, lenders, and managers rely on these reports to make important decisions. Consistency across statements reassures them that the numbers reflect real financial activity.

When discrepancies appear, they often point to recording errors, missing adjustments, or incorrect classifications.

Maintaining alignment between statements is therefore both a technical requirement and a practical safeguard.

It ensures that the financial picture presented by the reports is coherent and trustworthy.

READING FINANCIAL REPORTS AS A COMPLETE SYSTEM

Once someone becomes comfortable with the relationships between financial statements, reading them as a complete system becomes much easier.

Instead of viewing each report separately, the reader starts to move between them naturally.

A profit figure on the income statement leads to a look at the cash flow statement to see how much cash was actually generated. A large asset purchase on the balance sheet prompts a check of the investing section of the cash flow statement. Rising liabilities might lead to questions about financing activities or operational costs.

This integrated reading approach provides a more realistic understanding of the business.

For example, imagine analyzing a small technology startup.

The income statement shows modest revenue but growing losses due to heavy research and development spending. The cash flow statement reveals significant financing inflows from investors. The balance sheet shows increasing assets such as equipment and intellectual property.

Viewed separately, these numbers might seem confusing. Together, they describe a company investing heavily in future growth while relying on investor funding to support operations.

In another example, a family-owned manufacturing company might show steady profit on the income statement, strong operating cash flow, and a balance sheet with moderate debt and growing equity. Reading the statements together suggests a stable business generating reliable income and building long-term value.

Financial statements become most powerful when they are treated as parts of a larger system rather than isolated reports.

They reveal how the business earns money, how it uses that money, and how its financial structure evolves over time.

This interconnected view turns financial accounting into something far more practical than a set of formulas or technical rules. It becomes a framework for understanding how businesses operate, grow, and sustain themselves in the real world.

CHAPTER 16

HOW TO READ FINANCIAL STATEMENTS

Numbers on a financial statement can look impressive or intimidating depending on how familiar you are with them. Rows of figures, totals, and headings might seem like a foreign language at first glance. But financial statements are not meant to confuse people. Their purpose is the opposite. They are designed to bring clarity to the financial life of a business.

Learning how to read financial statements is similar to learning how to read a map. At first, the symbols and directions may look unfamiliar. After some practice, the map becomes a powerful tool. You begin to see where you are, where you are going, and what obstacles might lie ahead.

Financial statements serve the same purpose for a business. They reveal patterns, strengths, weaknesses, and opportunities that might otherwise remain hidden behind day-to-day activity. A business may appear busy and successful on the surface, but careful reading of its financial reports might tell a very different story.

Understanding how to read these reports is one of the most valuable skills for anyone involved in business. Entrepreneurs use it to make decisions. Managers use it to evaluate performance. Investors use it to judge whether a company is worth supporting. Even employees and consultants benefit from understanding how the organization they work with is performing financially.

Reading financial statements is not about memorizing formulas or performing complicated calculations. It is about learning to ask thoughtful questions and paying attention to the relationships between numbers. When you start reading reports with curiosity instead of fear, the numbers begin to make sense.

A well-prepared financial statement is more than a collection of figures. It is a story about how a business operates, how efficiently it uses its resources, and how effectively it turns effort into financial results.

IDENTIFYING FINANCIAL STRENGTHS

One of the first things readers look for in financial statements is evidence that a business is doing well. Strength in financial reporting can appear in several forms, and recognizing these signs helps build confidence in the company's stability.

A common sign of financial strength is **consistent profitability**. When a business reports steady or improving profits over time, it suggests that its products or services are valued in the marketplace and that its operations are being managed effectively. Consistency matters more than occasional spikes. A company that earns modest but reliable profits often stands on firmer ground than one that swings wildly between gains and losses.

Another sign of strength appears in the balance sheet. A business with **healthy assets compared to its liabilities** usually has more financial flexibility. If assets significantly exceed debts, the company may be better positioned to handle unexpected expenses or economic downturns.

Liquidity is another important indicator. Liquidity refers to the ability of a business to meet short-term obligations. If the company holds sufficient cash or easily convertible assets, it can pay suppliers, employees, and other obligations without financial strain.

Strong operating cash flow is another encouraging signal. When a business generates cash from its everyday activities, it demonstrates that the company's core operations are working effectively.

Revenue is not just appearing on paper; it is translating into real financial resources.

Financial strength can also be visible through **controlled expenses.** Businesses that manage costs carefully often maintain stable profit margins even when market conditions change. This discipline suggests strong internal management.

For example, imagine two small manufacturing companies. Both generate similar sales, but one consistently maintains lower operating costs and stronger cash flow. Over time, that company will likely build more financial resilience. Its ability to handle fluctuations in demand or rising costs will be stronger.

Recognizing these strengths in financial statements helps readers see beyond surface impressions. Instead of relying on guesswork, they can evaluate a business based on evidence.

RECOGNIZING WARNING SIGNS IN FINANCIAL REPORTS

Financial statements not only highlight strengths; they can also reveal potential problems. Spotting these warning signs early allows business owners and managers to address issues before they grow more serious.

One common warning sign is **declining profitability**. If revenue remains stable but profits shrink, it may indicate rising costs or inefficient operations. Businesses that ignore shrinking margins often find themselves struggling later.

Another signal appears when expenses grow faster than revenue. This pattern suggests that the business may be losing control over its cost structure. If left unchecked, rising expenses can slowly erode profitability even when sales look strong.

Cash flow problems can also signal trouble. A business may report healthy profits while experiencing constant cash shortages. This situation often arises when customers take too long to pay or when inventory purchases consume too much cash. Persistent cash flow pressure can eventually limit the company's ability to operate smoothly.

The balance sheet can also reveal warning signs. Rapidly increasing debt compared to assets may indicate that the company is relying heavily on borrowing. While debt can support growth, excessive borrowing creates financial risk.

Another red flag appears when accounts receivable grow faster than revenue. This pattern may suggest that customers are delaying payments or that the company's credit policies are too loose. Either situation can create cash flow stress.

For example, imagine a small retail business whose sales increase by ten percent, but its accounts receivable increase by forty percent. That difference suggests customers are paying much more slowly than before. Even though revenue looks strong, the business may soon face cash shortages.

Recognizing warning signs does not mean the business is failing. Instead, these signals serve as early alerts that adjustments may be needed. Financial reports act like diagnostic tools that help identify problems before they become severe.

INTERPRETING REVENUE AND PROFIT TRENDS

Revenue and profit are often the most closely watched numbers in financial reporting. Yet the real insight comes from studying how these figures change over time.

A single number tells only part of the story. A business might earn $100,000 in revenue this year, but without context it is difficult to know whether that result represents growth or decline. Comparing results across several periods reveals much more.

Revenue trends show whether demand for the company's products or services is increasing, decreasing, or remaining stable. Steady revenue growth often suggests that the business has found a reliable market and continues to attract customers.

However, revenue growth alone is not enough. Profit trends provide additional insight. If revenue rises but profits remain flat, it may indicate that expenses are increasing at the same rate as sales. In that case, the business is working harder without gaining additional financial benefit.

Healthy businesses usually aim for **balanced growth**, where both revenue and profit increase over time. This pattern suggests that the company is expanding while maintaining efficiency.

Profit trends also help identify seasonal patterns. Some businesses experience predictable cycles throughout the year. Retail stores often see stronger revenue during holiday seasons, while tourism businesses may experience peak periods during certain months.

By studying revenue and profit trends across multiple periods, readers can begin to see whether performance is improving, stagnating, or deteriorating.

For example, imagine a consulting firm whose revenue increases steadily for three years. If profits also grow during that time, it suggests that the firm is scaling successfully. If profits remain unchanged despite rising revenue, the firm may need to examine its cost structure.

Financial trends tell a story about momentum. They reveal whether the business is moving forward, standing still, or drifting backward.

UNDERSTANDING EXPENSE PATTERNS

Expenses are often overlooked when people first examine financial reports. Many readers focus primarily on revenue and profit, but expenses deserve equal attention. How a business spends money often reveals as much about its management as how it earns money.

Every business has a unique expense structure. Some industries require large investments in equipment or materials, while others rely mainly on labor or specialized expertise. Understanding these patterns helps explain why certain businesses operate differently from others.

Expense patterns become particularly important when analyzing changes over time. If expenses grow rapidly while revenue remains stable, the business may be facing operational inefficiencies. On the other hand, if expenses remain stable while revenue increases, the company may be improving its efficiency.

Certain expenses also deserve closer attention because they can fluctuate significantly. Marketing costs, for instance, may rise when a business launches a new campaign or enters a new market. Technology expenses may increase when a company upgrades its systems.

Fixed expenses, such as rent or insurance, tend to remain stable over time. Variable expenses, like raw materials or sales commissions, change with business activity. Understanding the difference between these types of costs helps readers interpret financial results more accurately.

For example, consider a small restaurant reviewing its financial reports. If food costs rise significantly while menu prices remain unchanged, profit margins may shrink. Identifying this trend early allows the owner to adjust purchasing strategies or pricing decisions.

Expense analysis also helps highlight opportunities for improvement. Sometimes small adjustments—such as renegotiating supplier contracts or improving inventory management—can significantly reduce costs.

By paying attention to expense patterns, readers gain a clearer understanding of how efficiently the business operates.

USING FINANCIAL STATEMENTS TO ASK BETTER QUESTIONS

Financial statements are not meant to provide all the answers. Their real value lies in helping readers ask better questions.

Numbers alone rarely explain why something happened. They simply reveal what happened. Once the numbers are visible, thoughtful questions can uncover the underlying causes.

For example, a reader might notice that revenue increased significantly during the year. That observation leads naturally to further questions. Did the business attract new customers, or did existing customers spend more? Was the increase driven by marketing efforts, price changes, or expanded services?

Similarly, a sudden increase in expenses might prompt questions about operational changes. Did the business hire additional staff? Invest in new equipment? Launch a marketing campaign?

Financial statements guide this process of inquiry. They provide the starting point for deeper investigation.

Consider a manager reviewing quarterly results. The income statement shows lower profits than expected. Instead of reacting immediately, the manager examines the expense categories and notices that advertising costs increased sharply. Further discussion reveals that the company recently launched a promotional campaign. The temporary increase in expenses now makes sense.

Another example might involve declining cash balances. By examining the cash flow statement, the reader might discover that the company invested heavily in new equipment during the period. The decrease in cash reflects strategic investment rather than financial trouble.

These examples highlight an important idea: financial statements do not replace judgment. They support it.

Good financial analysis combines numerical information with thoughtful interpretation. Readers who approach financial reports with curiosity and critical thinking gain far more insight than those who simply glance at totals.

Over time, this habit of asking questions transforms financial statements from static documents into practical decision-making tools.

Business leaders, investors, and analysts often develop a routine when reviewing financial reports. They scan for major changes, compare results across periods, and look for relationships between different numbers. Each observation leads to further questions that deepen their understanding of the business.

When used in this way, financial statements become far more than accounting documents. They become guides for understanding how a business operates, how it performs under different conditions, and where its future opportunities and challenges may lie.

CHAPTER 17

BASIC FINANCIAL ANALYSIS

Once someone becomes comfortable reading financial statements, a natural next step is learning how to **analyze** them. Reading tells you what the numbers are. Analysis helps explain what those numbers mean.

A business might report strong revenue, but does that revenue translate into healthy profit? Another company might hold significant assets, but are those assets being used efficiently? Two businesses may earn similar profits, yet one may be far more stable financially than the other.

Financial analysis helps answer questions like these.

At its core, financial analysis is the process of studying financial statements in order to understand the condition and performance of a business. It looks beyond individual numbers and focuses on patterns, relationships, and trends. The goal is not simply to observe what happened but to understand **why it happened and what it suggests about the future**.

Many people assume financial analysis is complicated, filled with advanced formulas or technical calculations. In reality, the basic ideas are straightforward. A few simple indicators and ratios can reveal a great deal about how a business operates.

Small business owners often perform financial analysis without realizing it. When they compare last month's profit to this month's profit, they are analyzing performance. When they check whether cash reserves are enough to cover upcoming expenses, they are evaluating financial stability. Financial analysis simply turns those instincts into a more structured approach.

Understanding these principles allows anyone—whether a student, entrepreneur, or manager—to interpret financial reports with greater confidence. Instead of seeing a page of numbers, they begin to see patterns, opportunities, and potential risks.

WHY FINANCIAL ANALYSIS MATTERS

Financial statements provide valuable information, but the numbers themselves do not automatically reveal what is good, bad, or normal. A profit figure of $50,000 may sound impressive until you learn that the company generated $2 million in revenue. In that case, the profit margin might actually be quite thin.

Financial analysis helps place numbers in context.

Businesses operate in dynamic environments where decisions must often be made quickly. Managers need to know whether performance is improving, whether expenses are under control, and whether the business can handle unexpected challenges. Financial analysis transforms raw numbers into insights that guide these decisions.

Investors rely on financial analysis to determine whether a company is worth supporting. Lenders use it to assess whether a borrower can repay a loan. Business owners use it to evaluate whether their strategies are producing the desired results.

Consider a small retail store reviewing its financial reports. The income statement shows steady revenue growth, but the owner notices that profits have not increased. Financial analysis may reveal that operating expenses have grown at the same pace as revenue. That insight encourages the owner to investigate cost control and operational efficiency.

Financial analysis also helps identify trends over time. A single financial report provides only a snapshot. When multiple periods are compared, patterns begin to emerge. Revenue may show steady growth, expenses may fluctuate seasonally, or profits may reveal a gradual upward trend.

These patterns provide valuable information about how the business is evolving.

Another important benefit of financial analysis is its ability to highlight risks. Declining profit margins, rising debt levels, or shrinking cash reserves may signal that a business needs to adjust its strategy. Early detection allows managers to take corrective action before problems become severe.

Ultimately, financial analysis turns financial statements into practical tools. Instead of simply recording history, the numbers become guides for making better decisions about the future.

PROFITABILITY INDICATORS

Profitability is one of the most important aspects of financial analysis. Businesses exist to create value, and profit is one of the clearest signs that the organization is succeeding in that goal.

Profitability indicators help measure how effectively a company converts revenue into earnings.

One of the simplest measures is **gross profit margin**. This indicator compares gross profit to total revenue and shows how much money remains after covering the direct cost of producing goods or services.

Gross profit margin is calculated as:

Gross Profit ÷ Revenue

Suppose a company earns $100,000 in revenue and reports $40,000 in gross profit. This means that forty percent of each dollar of revenue remains after covering the direct costs of production.

A higher gross margin often indicates that the business has strong pricing power or efficient production processes. A declining margin may suggest rising costs or competitive pressure on pricing.

Another useful measure is **net profit margin**. This ratio examines how much profit remains after all expenses have been deducted from revenue.

Net Profit ÷ Revenue

If a business earns $10,000 in net income from $100,000 in revenue, the net profit margin is ten percent. This means the company keeps ten cents of every dollar earned after covering all costs.

Net margin is especially important because it reflects the overall efficiency of the business. It captures not only production costs but also operating expenses, interest, and taxes.

Profitability can also be viewed in relation to assets. A company may own valuable resources, but those resources must generate returns in order to justify their use.

Return on assets measures how efficiently a business uses its assets to generate profit.

Net Income ÷ Total Assets

A higher return on assets suggests that the business is using its resources effectively. A lower return may indicate that assets are underutilized or that the company is carrying more assets than necessary.

For example, imagine two companies that each earn $20,000 in profit. If one company uses $200,000 in assets while the other uses $400,000, the first company is generating the same profit with fewer resources.

From an efficiency standpoint, that company may be performing better.

Profitability indicators help answer an essential question: **Is the business turning its effort and resources into meaningful financial results?**

LIQUIDITY AND FINANCIAL STABILITY

Profitability tells part of the story, but a profitable business can still face financial trouble if it cannot meet its short-term obligations. Liquidity refers to a company's ability to pay its bills on time.

Liquidity analysis focuses on whether the business has enough current assets—such as cash, receivables, and inventory—to cover its short-term liabilities.

One commonly used measure is the **current ratio**.

Current Assets ÷ Current Liabilities

If a business has $50,000 in current assets and $25,000 in current liabilities, the current ratio is 2. This means the company has twice as many short-term resources as short-term obligations.

A higher current ratio generally indicates greater financial flexibility. It suggests that the business can comfortably meet upcoming payments.

However, extremely high ratios may also signal inefficiency. Excess cash sitting idle or large amounts of unsold inventory may indicate that resources are not being used productively.

Another liquidity measure is the **quick ratio**, sometimes called the acid-test ratio. This ratio focuses on the most liquid assets, excluding inventory.

(Cash + Accounts Receivable) ÷ Current Liabilities

The quick ratio provides a more conservative view of liquidity because inventory may not always be easily converted into cash.

Liquidity analysis is especially important for businesses operating in industries with tight cash cycles. Restaurants, retail stores, and construction firms often face significant short-term expenses, making careful cash management essential.

Financial stability extends beyond short-term liquidity. Long-term stability depends on maintaining a healthy balance between assets, liabilities, and equity.

A company that relies heavily on borrowed money may face greater risk if economic conditions change. On the other hand, a business with strong equity and moderate debt may be better positioned to handle uncertainty.

Evaluating both liquidity and stability helps determine whether a business is financially resilient.

SIMPLE FINANCIAL RATIOS EXPLAINED

Financial ratios are tools that help transform raw numbers into meaningful comparisons. They allow readers to evaluate performance, efficiency, and stability in a consistent way.

Although many ratios exist, beginners can gain valuable insight from a small number of simple ones.

The **gross margin ratio** compares gross profit to revenue and reveals how efficiently the business produces goods or services.

Gross Profit ÷ Revenue

The **net profit margin** measures overall profitability after all expenses have been deducted.

Net Income ÷ Revenue

The **current ratio** evaluates liquidity by comparing current assets with current liabilities.

Current Assets ÷ Current Liabilities

Another useful measure is the **debt-to-equity ratio**, which compares total liabilities to owner's equity.

Total Liabilities ÷ Equity

This ratio shows how much of the business is financed through borrowing versus owner investment.

A higher debt-to-equity ratio suggests greater reliance on debt. While borrowing can support growth, excessive debt may increase financial risk.

The **asset turnover ratio** measures how effectively a business uses its assets to generate revenue.

Revenue ÷ Total Assets

This ratio is particularly useful when comparing businesses in asset-intensive industries. It reveals whether assets are being used efficiently to produce sales.

Ratios become most powerful when they are compared over time or against industry averages. A ratio that appears strong in one industry might be considered weak in another.

For example, grocery stores often operate with lower profit margins but higher sales volume, while consulting firms may have higher margins with lower sales volume.

Understanding these differences helps ensure that financial analysis remains realistic and meaningful.

INTERPRETING FINANCIAL PERFORMANCE

Numbers alone rarely provide complete answers. Interpreting financial performance requires combining numerical analysis with thoughtful judgment.

A single ratio or indicator rarely tells the whole story. Instead, analysts look for patterns across multiple measures and over several periods.

Consider a business that reports increasing revenue but declining profit margins. This pattern might indicate rising production costs or inefficient operations. Alternatively, it could reflect strategic decisions to lower prices in order to gain market share.

Similarly, a company with strong profit margins but declining sales may face competitive pressure or changing consumer preferences.

Interpreting financial performance often involves asking deeper questions about the business environment.

Are customers becoming more loyal, or is the company relying on heavy discounts to maintain sales? Are operating expenses increasing because of expansion, or because of poor cost control? Is the company investing in future growth, or struggling to maintain current operations?

For example, a technology startup may show negative profits during its early years because it is investing heavily in product development. In that context, losses may not necessarily signal failure. Instead, they may reflect a strategy focused on long-term growth.

On the other hand, a mature company with declining profits and rising debt may face more serious challenges.

Financial performance should also be evaluated relative to the company's goals and industry conditions. A ten percent profit margin may be excellent in one industry but modest in another.

Successful analysis balances quantitative information with qualitative understanding.

Over time, readers become more comfortable interpreting financial statements. Patterns that once seemed confusing begin to reveal clear signals about how the business is performing.

Financial analysis ultimately transforms financial statements into a powerful decision-making resource. By examining profitability, liquidity, efficiency, and trends, readers gain a deeper understanding of the forces shaping the financial health of a business.

CHAPTER 18

PROFIT VS. CASH FLOW

Few things confuse new business owners more than this: the business looks profitable on paper, yet the bank account feels painfully tight.

Sales are coming in. Invoices are being sent. The income statement shows a profit. Still, there is stress about rent, salaries, supplier payments, and next week's bills. It feels contradictory at first, almost unfair. If the business is profitable, why does money still feel scarce?

The answer lies in the difference between **profit** and **cash flow**.

Profit is a measure of performance. It tells you whether revenue was greater than expenses over a period of time. Cash flow is about movement. It tells you when money actually entered and left the business. Those are related ideas, but they are not identical. A business can be profitable and short on cash. It can also have strong cash for a while even when profit is weak.

This difference matters more than many beginners realize. A business can survive temporary dips in profit if it has enough cash and control. But if it runs out of cash, operations can become shaky very quickly. Staff still need to be paid. Suppliers still expect money. Utilities, rent, transport, subscriptions, and taxes do not pause just because a business is "profitable in theory."

That is why experienced business owners often pay close attention to both the income statement and the cash flow situation. Profit shows whether the model is working. Cash flow shows whether the business can keep breathing while it works.

Once you understand the gap between these two ideas, many financial puzzles begin to make sense. Delayed customer payments, inventory purchases, loan repayments, advance expenses, and timing differences all become easier to understand. Instead of asking only, "Did we make a profit?" you start asking a more grounded question: "Do we actually have enough cash to operate well?"

That is the kind of question that keeps businesses alive.

WHY PROFIT DOES NOT ALWAYS MEAN CASH

Profit and cash often move in the same general direction, but they do not move at the same speed, and they do not always arrive at the same time.

Profit is based on accounting rules that match revenue and expenses to the period in which they were earned or incurred. Cash, on the other hand, only changes when money actually comes in or goes out. This timing difference is the source of much confusion.

Imagine a small event planner who completes a wedding package worth $4,000 in June. Under proper accounting, that revenue belongs to June because the service was delivered in June. So the income statement records the revenue right away. But what if the client does not pay until July? June shows the profit, yet the cash has not arrived. The business may look stronger on paper than it feels in the bank.

Now turn to the expense side. Suppose that same event planner pays $1,200 upfront for a six-month software and marketing subscription. The cash leaves immediately, but the accounting treatment may spread the expense over time if part of it is prepaid. In other words, the cash may disappear in one month while the expense is recognized gradually. Again, profit and cash move on different schedules.

Inventory creates another common gap. A retail store might spend a large amount of cash buying stock in advance for the holiday season. The cash goes out immediately. But the cost only becomes an expense when the items are sold. So the business may feel the cash strain long before the income statement reflects the cost as cost of goods sold.

Loan payments also create a disconnect. If a business repays part of a loan, cash leaves the business. But only the interest portion usually affects profit as an expense. The principal repayment reduces a liability on the balance sheet, not profit on the income statement. So cash falls, but profit does not fall by the same amount.

Depreciation works in the opposite direction. It reduces profit because it is recorded as an expense, but it does not use up cash in the current period. The cash was spent earlier when the asset was purchased. That means profit may appear lower even though no money left the bank this month for that expense.

These differences are why someone can look at net income and still not understand why cash feels tight.

Net income is important, but it is not a live bank balance. It is a performance measure shaped by timing, recognition rules, and matching principles.

A useful way to think about it is this: profit tells you whether the business created value during the period. Cash tells you whether money actually moved in a way that supports survival and flexibility.

Both matter. But mistaking one for the other is one of the quickest ways to become financially blindsided.

HOW CASH FLOW AFFECTS BUSINESS SURVIVAL

Cash flow affects survival because bills live in the real world, not in theory.

A supplier is not comforted by the fact that your receivables are rising. A landlord does not accept "projected future revenue" in place of rent. Employees cannot take a promise of eventual profitability home as salary. When obligations are due, cash is what matters.

That is why a business can look decent on paper and still be in danger. If cash comes in too slowly or goes out too quickly, the business can become fragile even while reporting accounting profit.

Consider a small wholesale food business. It sells to restaurants and hotels on 30-day payment terms. Sales are strong, and the income statement looks healthy. But the business must pay farmers, transporters, fuel costs, and cold storage expenses almost immediately. If customer collections are delayed, the company can hit a cash crunch fast. It may be profitable in principle, but without available cash, operations begin to wobble.

This is one reason so many businesses struggle during growth. Growth often sounds positive, but it can consume cash. More sales may require more inventory, more packaging, more labor, more fuel, and more credit to customers. If the cash tied up in growth expands faster than the cash collected, the business can become financially stressed at the very moment it appears to be succeeding.

Cash flow also shapes freedom. A business with reliable cash flow can handle surprises, seize opportunities, and negotiate from a position of strength. It can stock up at a discount, invest in equipment, hire help when needed, or survive a slow month without panic. A business with weak cash flow is forced into reactive decisions. It delays payments, turns down opportunities, makes rushed borrowing choices, and spends too much energy trying to stay afloat.

There is also a mental and emotional side to this. Cash pressure creates tension. Owners who are constantly juggling urgent payments often lose the space needed for thoughtful strategy. Instead of planning growth, they are putting out fires. Instead of improving systems, they are worrying about tomorrow's balance. Over time, that pressure affects decision-making, confidence, and even the culture of the business.

This is why cash flow management is not just an accounting issue. It is an operating issue, a leadership issue, and sometimes a survival issue.

A business does not need to be perfect with cash to succeed. But it does need enough control and awareness to avoid becoming trapped by its own growth, delays, or commitments. Profit may describe success. Cash flow often determines whether the business can stay alive long enough to enjoy it.

UNDERSTANDING LIQUIDITY

Liquidity is the business's ability to meet its short-term obligations without falling into financial strain.

Put more simply, liquidity asks: **Can this business get its hands on enough usable money soon enough to pay what needs to be paid?**

This is slightly different from profitability. A business may be profitable overall but still have poor liquidity if too much of its value is tied up in inventory, unpaid invoices, or long-term assets. On the other hand, a business might have healthy liquidity for a while because it has cash on hand, even if profits are currently weak.

Cash itself is the most liquid asset because it is already available. Accounts receivable may be fairly liquid if customers pay soon. Inventory is less liquid because it first needs to be sold, and sometimes discounted, before it becomes cash. Equipment and buildings are even less liquid because they are not meant to be sold quickly in normal operations.

This is why balance sheets often separate current assets from non-current assets. Current assets are expected to turn into cash or be used within a shorter period, often within a year. They matter a great deal when thinking about liquidity.

Current liabilities matter too. These are the obligations due relatively soon, such as supplier balances, wages payable, taxes payable, short-term loans, and other near-term commitments.

When people talk about a business being “liquid enough,” they usually mean it has enough current resources to cover those near-term obligations without distress.

Imagine two businesses with the same total assets of $100,000.

The first has:

- $35,000 in cash
- $20,000 in receivables
- $15,000 in inventory
- $30,000 in equipment

The second has:

- $3,000 in cash
- $5,000 in receivables
- $12,000 in inventory
- $80,000 in equipment

On paper, both have the same total assets. But their liquidity is very different. The first business has much more flexibility to handle short-term payments. The second may struggle if several bills arrive at once.

Liquidity matters because business pressure often shows up first in the short term. Payroll is due this week. Supplier payment is due on Friday. The utility company expects payment now, not next quarter. If the business cannot respond, tension rises quickly.

Good liquidity gives breathing room. It allows the business to absorb delays, seasonal dips, and ordinary surprises. Weak liquidity makes everything harder.

This does not mean every business should hoard cash endlessly. Idle money has its own cost. But businesses need enough accessible resources to operate without constant strain. Liquidity is the difference between financial movement that feels controlled and financial movement that feels like a scramble.

MANAGING CASH EFFECTIVELY

Managing cash effectively is not just about having more money. It is about controlling the timing, visibility, and discipline around cash movement.

A business can improve its cash position in many ways without suddenly doubling its sales. Sometimes the biggest improvement comes from tighter habits rather than bigger revenue.

One of the most important habits is **watching customer collections closely**. A sale is only fully helpful when it turns into cash. Businesses that give credit to customers need to know who owes what, how long they have owed it, and which patterns are becoming dangerous. Following up on overdue invoices early is often easier than trying to recover them after months of silence.

Another important habit is **planning payments rather than reacting to them.** When owners know what major payments are due and when, they can prepare instead of scrambling. A simple cash calendar can reduce a surprising amount of stress. Seeing next week's obligations clearly often leads to better decisions this week.

Inventory control also matters. Too much inventory can quietly trap cash. A business may feel proud of full shelves, but if those products move slowly, money is being locked away instead of staying available for rent, salaries, or opportunity. Buying stock with more discipline often improves cash flow more than people expect.

Expense timing matters as well. Not every cost is equally urgent. Some expenses are essential to keep the business functioning. Others are optional or can be delayed without harming the operation. Effective cash management means knowing the difference.

There is also value in keeping a cash buffer whenever possible. Businesses rarely regret having some extra breathing room. Delayed payments, emergency repairs, price increases, equipment breakdowns, or seasonal slowdowns can all hit at inconvenient times. A small reserve can turn a crisis into an inconvenience.

Good cash management also involves separating personal and business finances. This is especially important for freelancers and small business owners. When personal withdrawals happen casually and unpredictably, it becomes harder to see what the business truly needs. Clear boundaries make cash decisions much more reliable.

Forecasting can help too. A cash forecast does not need to be complicated. It can be as simple as estimating what cash is expected to come in over the next few weeks and what major payments are due in the same period. Even a basic forecast makes the future feel less foggy.

Technology helps, but it does not replace discipline. Accounting software can track balances, send invoice reminders, and generate reports. Those tools are useful. But the habits behind them still matter. Looking at the reports regularly, acting on warning signs, and making thoughtful decisions remain the human part of the work.

At its best, cash management creates calm. It reduces the number of emergency decisions. It gives the owner a clearer view of what is possible, what is risky, and what needs attention now. That kind of clarity is worth far more than many beginners realize.

REAL-WORLD CASH FLOW SCENARIOS

Cash flow becomes easier to understand when you see it in situations that sound like real life rather than textbook diagrams.

Consider a small furniture maker. Business is growing well, and orders are coming in faster than before. On the income statement, the company looks strong. But to fulfill the extra demand, the owner buys more wood, hardware, and finishing materials upfront. Customers pay deposits, but full payment often comes only after delivery. In the meantime, the workshop pays staff, transport, rent, and utilities. The result is a growing business with growing pressure. Profit is real, but cash is under strain because growth is tying money up before collections catch up.

Now think about a freelance designer who lands several large projects in one quarter. Revenue looks excellent. Yet many of the clients are corporate and pay on 45-day terms. The designer also upgrades a laptop, renews software, and pays for advertising during the same period. So the income statement feels exciting, but the bank balance feels less exciting. The business is not failing. It is dealing with timing. Still, timing can hurt if ignored.

Take a neighborhood grocery store. Sales are mostly cash or immediate card payments, so collections are strong. That sounds healthy, and often it is. But suppose the owner overbuys perishable stock because of a holiday rush that does not fully materialize. Some inventory spoils. Cash was spent, but sales do not recover it. Here, the cash flow issue is not slow-paying customers. It is inventory discipline. The lesson is that cash pressure can come from different directions depending on the type of business.

Now consider a small school or training center. It receives tuition payments at the start of term, so cash looks abundant for a while. But staff salaries, facility costs, and maintenance continue month after month. If the school mistakes that early cash boost for long-term comfort and spends too freely, it may face a dry stretch before the next payment cycle. In this case, the danger is not weak revenue but poor pacing.

Another example is a service company that wins a major contract and decides to celebrate by hiring quickly, leasing a more expensive office, and increasing fixed costs. The new contract is real, but client payments arrive later than expected, and a second major contract does not materialize. Suddenly the business has committed to more monthly obligations than its cash flow can comfortably support. Here, the problem is not lack of opportunity. It is moving too aggressively before cash proved durable.

These scenarios show why cash flow management cannot rely on one simple rule. Different businesses face different patterns. Retail may struggle with stock control. Service businesses may struggle with receivables. Growing businesses may struggle with timing gaps. Seasonal businesses may struggle with pacing. Startup-style businesses may struggle with overcommitting before cash stabilizes.

What they all share is this: the movement of cash shapes what is realistically possible.

A business owner who understands that starts to view financial decisions differently. They think not only about profit, but about timing. Not only about growth, but about how growth is funded. Not only about sales, but about when those sales actually become usable money.

That shift in thinking is one of the marks of financial maturity. It is where accounting stops feeling like theory and starts feeling like practical judgment.

CHAPTER 19

COMMON ACCOUNTING MISTAKES BEGINNERS MAKE

Every new skill comes with a learning curve, and accounting is no exception. When people first begin managing financial records, small mistakes are almost unavoidable. Some errors come from misunderstanding basic concepts, while others happen because record keeping feels tedious and gets postponed until "later." Over time, these small issues can grow into bigger problems if they are not corrected early.

Fortunately, most beginner accounting mistakes follow recognizable patterns. Once you know what to watch for, it becomes much easier to avoid them. Many experienced business owners can look back and recall the early days of their businesses when they made similar missteps—mixing personal and business expenses, forgetting to record transactions, or assuming that strong sales automatically meant strong profits.

Understanding these common pitfalls is not meant to discourage anyone. Instead, it provides a practical roadmap. By recognizing the mistakes others have made, you can build better habits from the start.

Accounting works best when it becomes part of the regular rhythm of running a business. Clear records, careful classification, and regular review turn financial management from a stressful chore into a reliable source of insight. When the numbers are organized and accurate, they begin to answer important questions: Is the business profitable? Are expenses under control? Is cash flowing in at the right pace?

Many problems that appear mysterious or overwhelming later on often trace back to simple accounting habits that were neglected earlier. Taking the time to develop strong practices now can save a great deal of frustration in the future.

CONFUSING REVENUE WITH PROFIT

One of the most common misunderstandings in business occurs when people treat revenue and profit as if they mean the same thing. At first glance, it is easy to see why. Revenue represents the money coming into the business, and seeing large sales figures can feel encouraging.

However, revenue tells only half the story.

Profit is what remains after all expenses have been deducted from revenue. These expenses include the cost of goods, employee wages, rent, utilities, marketing, equipment costs, and many other operating expenses. If those costs are high, a business may generate impressive revenue while producing very little profit.

Consider a small online store that sells handmade accessories. During a busy holiday season, the store generates $50,000 in sales revenue. At first glance, the owner might feel thrilled with the result. But once the costs of materials, shipping, packaging, advertising, transaction fees, and labor are deducted, the actual profit might be closer to $8,000.

Revenue shows activity. Profit shows success.

This confusion can lead to poor decisions. A business owner might assume the company is thriving because sales are strong, even though expenses are rising at the same pace. Without carefully reviewing profit figures, the business may continue expanding costs without realizing how thin its margins have become.

Successful businesses keep a close eye on both numbers. Revenue reveals demand and market reach. Profit reveals efficiency and sustainability.

Recognizing the difference helps owners make more balanced decisions about pricing, production costs, and operational strategy.

MISCLASSIFYING EXPENSES

Another frequent beginner mistake occurs when expenses are placed in the wrong category. At first this may seem like a minor issue, but over time it can distort the financial picture of the business.

Accounting systems rely on organized categories to track how money is being spent. These categories might include rent, utilities, marketing, supplies, equipment, travel, or payroll. When expenses are recorded correctly, it becomes easy to see where the business is allocating its resources.

Problems arise when transactions are recorded under the wrong heading. For example, a business owner might record the purchase of a long-term asset—such as a computer or machine—as a simple office expense. In reality, that purchase may need to be treated as equipment and depreciated over time.

Similarly, advertising expenses might accidentally be recorded as general administrative costs, making it difficult to evaluate whether marketing efforts are delivering results.

Misclassification creates confusion when reviewing reports. If expenses appear to be rising in one category while falling in another, the change may reflect a recording error rather than a real shift in spending.

Imagine a café owner trying to evaluate food costs for the month. If some ingredient purchases were mistakenly recorded as general supplies, the reported food cost percentage may appear lower than it truly is. This could lead the owner to believe that kitchen operations are highly efficient when the data actually tells a different story.

Maintaining consistent expense categories ensures that financial reports reflect reality rather than accidental mislabeling.

IGNORING CASH FLOW

Many beginners focus heavily on profit while paying little attention to cash flow. This can lead to unpleasant surprises even when the business appears successful.

Cash flow tracks the movement of money in and out of the business. A company might record strong revenue and profit on its income statement, but if customers delay payments or inventory purchases require large upfront spending, cash balances may still shrink.

For example, imagine a small construction company that completes several projects and issues invoices totaling $100,000. From an accounting perspective, that revenue has been earned. However, if most clients take sixty days to pay, the company must still cover wages, equipment rentals, and material costs during that waiting period.

Without careful monitoring of cash flow, the company may struggle to meet its short-term obligations despite appearing profitable.

Ignoring cash flow also makes it difficult to plan for upcoming expenses. Businesses often face seasonal patterns where certain months are more profitable than others. Without reviewing cash flow reports, owners may not notice these patterns until financial pressure builds.

Monitoring cash flow regularly helps identify potential shortages before they become urgent. It allows businesses to adjust payment schedules, encourage faster customer payments, or temporarily slow certain expenses.

A profitable business with poor cash flow can experience serious difficulties. A business with steady cash flow, even with modest profits, often has far greater stability.

POOR RECORD KEEPING

Accounting relies heavily on accurate and organized records. When transactions are not recorded properly, financial statements quickly lose their reliability.

Poor record keeping can take many forms. Some businesses delay entering transactions until weeks later. Others lose receipts, forget to record small expenses, or rely on memory rather than documentation.

These habits create gaps in the financial record. Over time, those gaps make it difficult to understand how money is being spent or where profits are actually coming from.

For example, imagine a freelance photographer who purchases camera accessories, software subscriptions, travel supplies, and marketing materials throughout the year. If these purchases are not recorded consistently, the total cost of running the business may be underestimated.

At tax time or during financial reviews, missing records can cause confusion and extra work. Reconstructing transactions from bank statements or credit card histories often takes far more time than recording them correctly from the start.

Organized records also provide protection during audits or financial reviews. Receipts, invoices, and payment confirmations serve as evidence that transactions occurred as reported.

Many modern accounting tools make record keeping easier by allowing transactions to be recorded immediately using mobile devices or automated bank feeds. However, technology alone cannot solve the problem. Consistency remains the key.

Regularly updating financial records ensures that reports remain accurate and useful.

HOW TO AVOID COSTLY ACCOUNTING ERRORS

Preventing accounting mistakes does not require advanced training. In most cases, it comes down to developing a few reliable habits.

The first habit is reviewing financial records regularly. Waiting until the end of the month—or worse, the end of the year—to examine accounts increases the risk that errors will go unnoticed. Regular reviews make it easier to catch small mistakes before they grow into larger issues.

Another helpful practice is maintaining clear documentation. Keeping digital or physical copies of invoices, receipts, and contracts ensures that transactions can be verified later. Organized documentation also speeds up tax preparation and financial reporting.

Using consistent categories for income and expenses improves clarity in financial reports. When categories remain stable over time, comparisons between months or years become more meaningful.

Separating personal and business finances is equally important. Mixing personal purchases with business expenses makes it difficult to determine the true cost structure of the business. Dedicated business accounts and credit cards help maintain clear financial boundaries.

Many beginners also benefit from consulting professionals when necessary. An accountant or bookkeeper can review records periodically to ensure that transactions are being recorded correctly. Even occasional guidance can prevent costly misunderstandings.

Technology can also support accuracy. Accounting software reduces manual calculations, organizes financial data automatically, and generates reports that help identify unusual patterns.

Finally, developing a mindset of curiosity toward financial reports can make a significant difference. Instead of viewing accounting as a chore, treating it as a source of insight encourages regular engagement with the numbers.

When accounting systems are organized and accurate, financial reports become powerful tools rather than confusing documents. They reveal patterns, highlight opportunities, and support better decision-making across every part of the business.

Avoiding these common mistakes does not require perfection. It simply requires attention, consistency, and a willingness to learn from experience. Over time, these habits transform accounting from a source of frustration into a reliable guide for running a successful business.

CHAPTER 20

ACCOUNTING FOR SMALL BUSINESSES

Running a small business involves far more than delivering a product or service. Behind every sale, shipment, invoice, and payment lies a financial story that shapes the health of the business. Accounting is the system that captures that story and turns it into something useful.

For many entrepreneurs, accounting initially feels like an obligation rather than a tool. It can seem tedious compared to the excitement of building products, finding customers, or growing a brand. Yet the businesses that last longest are often the ones whose owners understand their numbers clearly.

Accounting provides visibility. It answers practical questions that matter every day: Is the business truly profitable? Are expenses under control? Is enough cash available to cover next month's costs? Are certain products or services performing better than others?

Without reliable financial records, these questions become difficult to answer. Decisions start relying on guesswork instead of evidence.

Small business accounting does not require complex formulas or specialized jargon. At its core, it involves consistently tracking what the business earns, what it spends, and what it owns or owes. When done well, accounting becomes a quiet but powerful ally. It helps entrepreneurs make confident decisions, manage growth responsibly, and avoid costly surprises.

The earlier a business builds strong accounting habits, the easier it becomes to maintain financial clarity as the company grows.

WHY ENTREPRENEURS MUST UNDERSTAND ACCOUNTING

Entrepreneurs often begin with passion for an idea—launching a café, starting a consulting practice, opening an online store, or building a creative service. Passion drives the early stages, but sustainability depends on financial awareness.

Understanding accounting allows entrepreneurs to see beyond day-to-day activity and evaluate the real condition of their business.

Imagine a new bakery that sells hundreds of pastries each day. The shop appears busy and customers seem happy. Without careful accounting, however, the owner might overlook rising ingredient costs, increased electricity usage, or packaging expenses that gradually reduce profit margins.

Accounting shines a light on these details.

When entrepreneurs understand their financial statements, they gain the ability to measure progress objectively. They can track whether revenue is growing, whether expenses are rising too quickly, and whether investments in equipment or marketing are producing results.

This understanding also strengthens decision-making. When considering whether to hire a new employee, expand into a larger location, or invest in advertising, financial information provides the evidence needed to weigh those choices carefully.

Accounting also builds credibility. Lenders, investors, and partners often require financial reports before committing to a business relationship. Entrepreneurs who maintain organized financial records demonstrate professionalism and reliability.

Perhaps most importantly, accounting gives business owners a sense of control. Instead of reacting to financial problems after they occur, they can identify trends early and adjust their strategies accordingly.

A business owner who understands accounting is better equipped to guide the business through both opportunities and challenges.

TRACKING REVENUE AND EXPENSES

At the heart of small business accounting lies a simple practice: carefully recording revenue and expenses.

Revenue represents the income the business earns from selling products or providing services. Every sale, whether paid immediately or invoiced for later payment, should be recorded clearly.

Tracking revenue accurately helps entrepreneurs understand how much money the business is generating and which activities contribute most to that income.

Consider a freelance graphic designer who works with multiple clients throughout the year. Some clients request logo design, others commission website layouts, and a few require ongoing marketing materials. By recording revenue from each type of service separately, the designer can quickly see which services generate the most income.

This information becomes valuable when deciding where to focus future effort.

Expenses deserve equal attention. Every business incurs costs in order to operate—materials, equipment, utilities, rent, software subscriptions, transportation, and many other items.

Recording these expenses consistently reveals how much it actually costs to run the business.

For example, a small landscaping company may spend money on fuel, equipment maintenance, fertilizer, and employee wages. Without tracking these expenses carefully, it becomes difficult to determine whether pricing is sufficient to cover costs and generate profit.

Expense tracking also helps identify opportunities to improve efficiency. If a particular expense category grows unexpectedly, the business owner can investigate the cause and consider adjustments.

One helpful habit is recording transactions regularly rather than waiting until the end of the month.

Frequent updates keep records accurate and prevent small details from being forgotten.

When revenue and expenses are recorded clearly, the income statement becomes a reliable reflection of how the business is performing.

MONITORING PROFITABILITY

Revenue alone does not determine the success of a business. What truly matters is whether the business generates enough profit to sustain operations and reward the effort invested.

Profitability measures the difference between income and expenses. Monitoring it regularly helps entrepreneurs understand whether their business model is working effectively.

A business that consistently earns profit can reinvest in growth, improve its services, and build financial resilience. A business that struggles to maintain profit may need to adjust pricing, control costs, or rethink certain activities.

Profitability analysis often begins with simple comparisons. Entrepreneurs can review monthly or quarterly reports to observe how profit changes over time.

For example, imagine a small clothing boutique reviewing its financial results for three consecutive months. Revenue remains stable, but profit gradually declines. A closer look reveals that shipping costs and packaging expenses have increased due to supplier price changes.

With this insight, the owner can renegotiate supplier contracts or adjust pricing to maintain profitability.

Profitability monitoring can also reveal which products or services contribute most to earnings. Some offerings may generate strong margins, while others require significant effort for relatively small returns.

Understanding these patterns helps entrepreneurs allocate their time and resources wisely.

Regularly reviewing profit ensures that growth remains sustainable rather than merely impressive on the surface.

KEEPING ORGANIZED FINANCIAL RECORDS

Organization is one of the most valuable habits in small business accounting. When financial records are structured and accessible, information becomes easier to interpret and decisions become more informed.

Organized records typically include several types of documents: invoices sent to customers, receipts from purchases, bank statements, payroll records, and contracts with suppliers or service providers.

Each document represents a piece of the financial story of the business.

When these records are stored systematically—either digitally or in well-labeled physical files—they create a reliable reference for future review. If questions arise about a particular transaction, the supporting document can be located quickly.

Digital tools have made organization easier than ever. Many accounting platforms allow receipts to be photographed and uploaded instantly, linking them directly to the corresponding transaction. This approach eliminates the need to search through piles of paper later.

Consistency is key. Recording transactions in the same way each time ensures that reports remain accurate and comparable.

Organized records also simplify tax preparation. Instead of scrambling to reconstruct financial activity at the end of the year, entrepreneurs can generate reports directly from their accounting system.

In addition, organized records demonstrate professionalism when interacting with lenders, investors, or accountants. Clear documentation shows that the business operates responsibly and values transparency.

Strong organization turns accounting from a stressful obligation into a reliable system that supports the entire operation.

BUILDING A SIMPLE ACCOUNTING SYSTEM

Many small business owners assume they need complicated accounting systems to manage their finances effectively. In reality, a simple and consistent system often works best, especially during the early stages of a business.

A basic accounting system begins with a dedicated business bank account. Separating business finances from personal finances creates clarity and prevents confusion when reviewing transactions.

Next comes a reliable method for recording transactions. This may involve accounting software, spreadsheets, or bookkeeping applications designed for small businesses. The goal is to capture each transaction accurately and categorize it appropriately.

Regular updates keep the system functioning smoothly. Setting aside time each week to review transactions and record new entries prevents records from falling behind.

Periodic financial reviews are equally important. Monthly reports such as the income statement, balance sheet, and cash flow statement provide valuable insights into the current condition of the business.

These reports help answer important questions: Is revenue growing? Are expenses stable? Is cash flow healthy?

As the business expands, the accounting system can evolve. Additional tools may be added for inventory tracking, payroll management, or financial forecasting. However, the core principles remain the same—accurate recording, organized documentation, and regular review.

Some entrepreneurs also benefit from professional support. An accountant or bookkeeper can provide guidance, ensure compliance with regulations, and offer insights that improve financial management.

The most effective accounting systems are not necessarily the most complex. They are the ones that the business owner understands and uses consistently.

When entrepreneurs maintain clear financial records and review them regularly, accounting becomes far more than a reporting requirement. It becomes a powerful tool for guiding growth, identifying opportunities, and building a business that can thrive for years to come.

CHAPTER 21

USING ACCOUNTING FOR BETTER DECISIONS

A business produces numbers every day. Sales receipts, supplier invoices, payroll records, inventory purchases, subscription fees, loan payments, marketing expenses, and customer deposits all leave traces in the accounting system. At first, these records may appear to be little more than paperwork required for taxes or reporting.

Yet the real value of accounting appears when those numbers begin guiding decisions.

Good financial information helps business owners understand what is actually happening beneath the surface of daily activity. It reveals whether growth is healthy or risky, whether prices are sustainable, and whether the business is moving toward stability or drifting toward trouble.

Many small businesses fail not because they lack customers, but because decisions are made without clear financial insight. Owners may expand too quickly, price their products incorrectly, or underestimate the real cost of operations. Accounting reduces that uncertainty.

Financial records show patterns. They reveal which products generate the strongest returns, which expenses are rising faster than expected, and whether cash reserves are improving or shrinking. When owners learn to read those patterns, accounting becomes less about bookkeeping and more about strategy.

A well-organized accounting system does not simply track the past. It becomes a tool for shaping the future of the business.

FINANCIAL DATA IN BUSINESS DECISIONS

Every important business decision carries financial consequences. Whether an owner is considering hiring a new employee, expanding into a larger location, launching a new product line, or investing in marketing, the decision ultimately affects revenue, expenses, and profitability.

Financial data provides the information needed to evaluate these choices carefully.

Imagine a small catering company that receives increasing demand for large corporate events. The owner begins considering whether to purchase additional kitchen equipment and hire extra staff. Without financial records, the decision might rely mostly on instinct. With accounting data, the owner can examine past revenue patterns, labor costs, and ingredient expenses to estimate whether the expansion would produce enough profit to justify the investment.

Financial reports also reveal the true cost of operations. Many expenses appear small individually but add up quickly over time. Software subscriptions, maintenance costs, utilities, and transportation expenses may quietly consume a significant portion of revenue.

When these costs are visible in financial reports, business owners can evaluate whether certain activities are truly worth their expense.

Financial data also helps identify opportunities. Suppose a small online retailer reviews its sales records and notices that one particular product category consistently generates higher profit margins than others. This insight might encourage the business to expand that category or invest in targeted marketing.

Decisions grounded in financial data tend to be more balanced and less reactive. Instead of relying entirely on optimism or caution, the business owner can evaluate the evidence presented by the numbers.

Over time, this habit of consulting financial data before making major decisions strengthens the stability and direction of the business.

BUDGETING BASICS

A budget is essentially a financial plan. It estimates how much money a business expects to earn and spend during a future period.

For beginners, budgeting may sound restrictive, but its real purpose is clarity. A well-prepared budget helps business owners anticipate upcoming expenses, prepare for seasonal changes, and maintain control over their financial resources.

Creating a budget begins with reviewing historical financial data. Previous income statements and expense reports provide valuable insight into typical revenue levels and operating costs.

Suppose a small fitness studio reviews its financial records from the previous year. Membership fees provide the majority of revenue, while rent, instructor wages, equipment maintenance, and marketing make up the largest expenses. Using this information, the owner can estimate expected revenue and expenses for the coming year.

Budgets rarely predict the future perfectly. Unexpected events always occur. However, having a financial plan helps the business respond to changes more effectively.

A budget also encourages discipline. When expenses begin to exceed planned levels, the owner can identify the issue early and adjust accordingly. Without a budget, rising costs might go unnoticed until profits have already declined.

Budgets can also guide investment decisions. If a business expects strong revenue during certain months, it may schedule equipment purchases or marketing campaigns during those periods. This approach helps maintain steady cash flow throughout the year.

Even a simple budget provides structure. By outlining expected revenue and expenses, the business gains a clearer understanding of what it must achieve financially to remain healthy.

PRICING AND PROFITABILITY

Setting the right price for a product or service is one of the most important decisions a business makes. Prices that are too high may discourage customers, while prices that are too low may fail to cover costs.

Accounting data plays a critical role in determining appropriate pricing.

Before establishing prices, business owners need to understand their cost structure. This includes direct costs, such as materials or production expenses, as well as indirect costs like rent, utilities, and administrative expenses.

Consider a small furniture workshop producing handcrafted tables. Each table requires wood, hardware, finishing materials, and several hours of skilled labor. In addition, the workshop pays rent for its space, electricity for machinery, and transportation costs for deliveries.

If the owner sets prices based only on material costs, the business may fail to cover these additional expenses.

Accounting records reveal the true cost of producing each item or service. Once those costs are understood, the owner can determine how much margin is needed to achieve a healthy profit.

Profit margins vary across industries, but every business must ensure that revenue comfortably exceeds total costs. When pricing decisions ignore accounting data, businesses often discover too late that their margins are too thin.

Pricing also interacts with customer demand. Some businesses choose higher prices with smaller sales volumes, while others operate with lower margins but higher sales volume. Accounting helps evaluate which approach works best for the specific business.

Regularly reviewing profitability ensures that pricing remains aligned with changing costs and market conditions.

EVALUATING BUSINESS GROWTH

Growth often feels like the ultimate goal for many entrepreneurs. Increasing sales, expanding customer bases, and opening new locations can create excitement and momentum. However, growth is only beneficial when it strengthens the financial health of the business.

Accounting helps determine whether growth is sustainable.

Revenue growth is usually the most visible indicator. When sales increase steadily over time, it suggests that the business is gaining market traction. However, growth must also be accompanied by careful cost management.

For example, a small delivery service may double its revenue by expanding into new areas. Yet if fuel costs, vehicle maintenance, and labor expenses increase even faster, the additional revenue may not produce meaningful profit.

Financial reports help identify whether growth is improving profitability or simply increasing workload.

Cash flow analysis also plays a role in evaluating growth. Rapid expansion often requires larger investments in inventory, equipment, or staff. If cash flow cannot support these investments, the business may struggle despite rising sales.

Balance sheet analysis provides another perspective. Growth often increases both assets and liabilities.

Reviewing these changes helps determine whether the company is building long-term value or accumulating excessive debt.

Healthy growth strengthens revenue, maintains profitability, and preserves financial stability. Accounting helps ensure that expansion remains a positive development rather than an unsustainable burden.

MANAGING FINANCIAL RISKS

Every business faces financial risks. Market conditions can change unexpectedly. Costs may rise due to inflation or supply disruptions. Customers may delay payments, or new competitors may enter the market.

Accounting provides early warning signals that help businesses respond to these risks before they become severe.

For instance, declining profit margins may indicate that production costs are increasing faster than sales prices. Without accounting data, this trend might remain hidden until profits disappear entirely.

Similarly, rising accounts receivable balances may signal that customers are taking longer to pay.

Monitoring this trend allows the business to strengthen credit policies or follow up more quickly on overdue invoices.

Debt levels also require careful attention. Borrowing can help finance growth, but excessive debt creates financial pressure. Accounting records help track loan balances, interest payments, and repayment schedules.

Cash reserves provide another layer of protection. Businesses with strong cash positions can weather temporary downturns more easily. Maintaining a financial cushion allows owners to navigate uncertainty without making rushed decisions.

Risk management does not mean avoiding all uncertainty. Instead, it means understanding the financial position of the business well enough to anticipate challenges and prepare for them.

When accounting information is reviewed regularly, risks become easier to identify and manage. Financial records reveal patterns that might otherwise remain unnoticed.

In this way, accounting becomes more than a reporting tool. It becomes a guide for navigating the complex financial landscape that every business must face.

CHAPTER 22

UNDERSTANDING FINANCIAL REPORTS AT WORK

In many workplaces, financial reports circulate quietly in the background. Managers review them during meetings, executives discuss them during planning sessions, and finance teams prepare them at the end of each reporting period. For employees who do not work directly in accounting, these reports may seem distant or overly technical.

Yet financial information influences far more decisions than many people realize.

Hiring plans, marketing budgets, product development, equipment purchases, salary adjustments, and expansion strategies often rely on the insights revealed in financial reports. These documents provide a snapshot of how the organization is performing and where it might be heading next.

Understanding financial reports does not require an accounting degree. Even a basic grasp of the numbers allows professionals in any department to participate more confidently in discussions about performance and strategy.

A project manager reviewing cost reports can identify opportunities to control spending. A marketing specialist analyzing campaign results can evaluate whether promotional investments are producing meaningful returns. A team leader examining department budgets can understand how daily operational decisions affect the broader financial picture.

Financial awareness strengthens communication across the workplace. Instead of viewing accounting reports as abstract documents produced by another department, employees begin to see them as tools that help explain how the organization operates.

When financial information becomes part of everyday thinking, decision-making becomes more informed and collaboration becomes more productive.

FINANCIAL REPORTS USED IN COMPANIES

Most companies rely on several core financial reports to monitor performance and guide decision-making. These reports provide different perspectives on the financial condition of the organization.

The income statement, sometimes called the profit and loss statement, summarizes revenue and expenses over a specific period. It shows whether the company generated a profit or experienced a loss. Managers often examine this report to evaluate how efficiently the company is converting sales into earnings.

The balance sheet presents a snapshot of the company's financial position at a particular moment. It lists assets, liabilities, and equity, revealing what the company owns, what it owes, and the value belonging to its owners or shareholders.

The cash flow statement focuses on the movement of cash in and out of the business. It explains how operating activities, investments, and financing decisions affect the company's cash position.

In addition to these core statements, companies often prepare internal reports tailored to specific departments or projects. For example, a manufacturing company may produce production cost reports that analyze the expenses involved in creating specific products. A retail company might generate sales reports that compare revenue across different store locations.

Budgets and forecasts also play a key role. These documents estimate future income and expenses, allowing managers to plan ahead and allocate resources effectively.

Together, these reports create a comprehensive financial picture. Each report highlights different aspects of performance, and when they are examined together, they provide a deeper understanding of how the organization operates.

HOW MANAGERS USE FINANCIAL DATA

Managers rely on financial data to evaluate performance, allocate resources, and make strategic decisions. The numbers recorded by the accounting system serve as evidence that supports or challenges management assumptions.

Consider a marketing manager reviewing a campaign that promoted a new product line. The campaign generated strong customer engagement online, but financial data reveals whether that interest translated into actual sales. If revenue from the product increased significantly during the campaign period, the manager may conclude that the strategy was effective.

Operations managers often use financial data to monitor efficiency. Production costs, labor expenses, and supply purchases all appear in accounting reports. By comparing these numbers across time periods, managers can identify trends that indicate improving or declining efficiency.

Financial data also guides budgeting decisions. Department leaders often receive budget allocations based on historical spending patterns and projected needs. Reviewing past financial performance helps ensure that resources are distributed in ways that support the company's goals.

In many organizations, managers also evaluate profitability at the product or service level. Some offerings generate higher margins than others. Understanding these differences helps companies decide where to invest their energy and resources.

For example, a software company might discover that one subscription package consistently produces higher profit margins than other offerings. Armed with this insight, management may choose to emphasize that package in future marketing campaigns.

Financial data transforms managerial decisions from guesswork into informed judgment.

PARTICIPATING IN FINANCIAL DISCUSSIONS

Financial discussions often occur during team meetings, strategy sessions, and performance reviews. For employees who are unfamiliar with accounting terminology, these conversations can sometimes feel intimidating.

However, participating effectively in financial discussions often requires only a basic understanding of the key reports and metrics being discussed.

When revenue figures are mentioned, it helps to understand that revenue reflects the income generated from sales. When profit margins appear in conversation, they refer to the portion of revenue that remains after covering costs. References to cash flow usually relate to how much money the company actually has available to fund operations.

Employees who understand these concepts can contribute valuable insights from their own areas of expertise.

For instance, a sales representative who understands revenue targets can offer feedback about customer demand and pricing trends. A project manager who understands cost reports can suggest ways to reduce unnecessary spending.

Financial discussions are rarely about numbers alone. They often involve interpreting those numbers in the context of real-world operations.

Suppose a team meeting reveals that production costs increased during the last quarter. Employees working in manufacturing might explain that raw material prices have risen or that equipment maintenance requirements have increased. Their operational knowledge helps management interpret the financial data accurately.

Participating in financial discussions becomes easier when employees approach the numbers with curiosity rather than hesitation. Asking thoughtful questions—such as why a particular expense increased or how a new initiative affected revenue—contributes to a deeper understanding for everyone involved.

UNDERSTANDING PERFORMANCE METRICS

Organizations frequently use performance metrics to evaluate how well different parts of the business are operating. These metrics translate financial data into measurable indicators that managers can monitor regularly.

One common metric is profit margin, which shows how much profit remains after covering expenses. A higher margin suggests greater efficiency in converting revenue into earnings.

Revenue growth is another widely used metric. Tracking revenue across multiple periods reveals whether the company's sales are expanding or declining.

Cost ratios provide insight into how expenses relate to revenue. For example, a company might examine the percentage of revenue spent on marketing or administrative costs. These ratios help managers determine whether spending levels are appropriate for the size of the business.

In manufacturing environments, metrics such as cost per unit or production efficiency often appear in financial reports. These measurements help companies evaluate whether production processes are operating smoothly.

Customer-related metrics also play an important role. Average revenue per customer, customer acquisition costs, and retention rates all influence financial performance.

Performance metrics are most useful when they are monitored consistently over time. A single measurement may not reveal much on its own, but patterns that develop across multiple periods provide valuable insight.

For example, if marketing expenses increase while revenue remains unchanged, the company may reconsider its promotional strategy. If revenue rises steadily while operating costs remain stable, management may conclude that the business is scaling efficiently.

Understanding these metrics helps employees recognize how their work contributes to the overall performance of the organization.

IMPROVING FINANCIAL AWARENESS IN THE WORKPLACE

Financial awareness strengthens organizations by encouraging employees to think about how their actions influence the company's financial results.

When employees understand the financial impact of their decisions, they often become more thoughtful about how resources are used. A purchasing manager may negotiate better supplier contracts. A project team may identify ways to reduce unnecessary expenses. A customer service department may recognize opportunities to improve customer retention, which ultimately supports revenue growth.

Organizations can encourage financial awareness by sharing relevant financial information with employees. Regular performance updates, department-level financial reports, and discussions about business goals help create a culture of transparency.

Training programs can also help employees develop a basic understanding of financial statements and business metrics. When people feel comfortable interpreting financial information, they are more likely to engage actively in discussions about performance.

Financial awareness also strengthens collaboration across departments. Marketing teams, operations managers, and finance professionals each bring different perspectives to the table. When everyone understands the financial implications of their work, decisions can be evaluated more effectively.

Over time, this shared understanding contributes to better planning, stronger accountability, and improved results.

Financial reports are not just tools for accountants or executives. They are guides that help every part of the organization understand where the business stands and how each team can contribute to its success.

CHAPTER 23

ACCOUNTING TOOLS AND TECHNOLOGY

Not long ago, accounting meant ledgers, paper receipts, and long hours of manual calculations. Bookkeepers would write entries by hand, update balances manually, and store documents in filing cabinets. The process worked, but it required patience, precision, and a great deal of time.

Today, technology has transformed how businesses manage their finances.

Modern accounting tools allow entrepreneurs and professionals to track transactions, generate reports, and monitor financial performance with far greater efficiency. What once took hours of careful calculation can now happen automatically within seconds.

Yet the purpose of accounting technology has not changed. These tools still perform the same fundamental task: recording financial activity and organizing it into useful information. The difference lies in how quickly and accurately that information can be processed.

Technology also helps reduce errors. Automated calculations, integrated bank feeds, and digital record storage make it easier to maintain accurate financial records. Instead of worrying about arithmetic mistakes or misplaced paperwork, business owners can focus more on understanding what the numbers reveal.

For beginners especially, accounting technology provides a valuable advantage. Many modern systems are designed with simplicity in mind. They guide users through the process of recording transactions and automatically generate financial statements that once required extensive bookkeeping knowledge.

However, technology is only as useful as the understanding behind it. Software can record numbers, but it cannot replace the judgment needed to interpret those numbers correctly. A strong grasp of accounting principles ensures that technology becomes a helpful assistant rather than a confusing black box.

When accounting knowledge and technology work together, financial management becomes far more manageable.

INTRODUCTION TO ACCOUNTING SOFTWARE

Accounting software is designed to help businesses record financial transactions, organize financial data, and produce reports that reveal the financial condition of the company.

At its most basic level, accounting software replaces traditional paper ledgers. Instead of manually writing journal entries and calculating balances, the system records transactions electronically and updates accounts automatically.

Most accounting platforms include several core features. They allow users to record sales, track expenses, create invoices, monitor payments from customers, and manage supplier bills. As these transactions are entered, the software organizes the data into financial statements such as the income statement, balance sheet, and cash flow statement.

One of the greatest advantages of accounting software is its ability to perform calculations instantly. When a transaction is recorded, the system automatically updates the relevant accounts. This reduces the risk of mathematical errors that sometimes occur in manual bookkeeping.

Another useful feature is report generation. With just a few clicks, users can view summaries of revenue, expenses, profit margins, and other financial metrics. These reports help business owners monitor performance without needing to calculate totals manually.

Accounting software also supports better organization. Digital systems store financial records in structured databases, making it easier to search for specific transactions or review historical data.

For beginners, the key benefit of accounting software lies in its ability to simplify complex tasks. By automating calculations and organizing financial information, these tools allow users to focus more on understanding their financial results rather than performing repetitive bookkeeping work.

DIGITAL BOOKKEEPING SYSTEMS

Digital bookkeeping systems extend beyond basic accounting software by integrating multiple aspects of financial management into a unified platform.

Traditional bookkeeping required several separate processes. Invoices were created manually, bank statements were reviewed separately, and receipts were stored in physical folders. Digital systems bring these elements together within a single environment.

One common feature of digital bookkeeping is **bank integration**. Many systems can connect directly to a business bank account and automatically import transactions. This reduces the need for manual entry and ensures that financial records stay up to date.

Once transactions are imported, users can categorize them into appropriate accounts such as office supplies, marketing expenses, or travel costs. Over time, the system may even learn to recognize recurring transactions and categorize them automatically.

Digital bookkeeping systems also make it easier to manage invoices. Businesses can create professional invoices directly within the platform and send them electronically to customers. When payments are received, the system records them automatically, updating accounts receivable balances.

Receipt management is another area where digital tools offer major improvements. Instead of keeping stacks of paper receipts, users can photograph documents with their phones and upload them directly into the accounting system. The receipts become attached to the corresponding transactions, creating a clear record for future reference.

These systems also improve collaboration. Accountants, bookkeepers, and business owners can access the same financial records from different locations. This makes it easier to review financial data, prepare reports, and resolve questions quickly.

Digital bookkeeping systems reduce administrative workload and improve the reliability of financial records. By simplifying the process of recording transactions, they allow businesses to maintain organized financial data with far less effort.

AUTOMATION IN MODERN ACCOUNTING

Automation has become one of the most powerful developments in modern accounting technology. Many tasks that once required manual effort can now be completed automatically through intelligent software systems.

One example is automatic transaction categorization. When a business connects its bank accounts to accounting software, transactions can be imported and categorized based on predefined rules. For instance, payments to a utility company may automatically be categorized as utilities expenses.

Recurring transactions can also be automated. Rent payments, subscription fees, and loan repayments often occur on predictable schedules. Accounting systems can record these transactions automatically at regular intervals.

Automation also simplifies invoice management. Some systems send payment reminders to customers when invoices become overdue. This feature reduces the time spent following up on unpaid accounts and helps improve cash flow.

Another powerful automation feature involves financial reporting. Instead of compiling reports manually at the end of each month, modern systems can generate real-time financial summaries whenever they are needed. Business owners can review revenue trends, expense patterns, and cash balances instantly.

Automation improves efficiency, but it also introduces an important responsibility. Users must still review transactions periodically to ensure that the system is categorizing them correctly. Technology reduces the workload, but human oversight remains essential.

When used thoughtfully, automation allows businesses to maintain accurate financial records while freeing up time for strategic thinking and decision-making.

CHOOSING THE RIGHT ACCOUNTING TOOLS

Selecting appropriate accounting tools depends on the size, complexity, and needs of the business. A freelancer managing a small consulting practice may require different tools than a retail company with multiple employees and inventory systems.

Several factors can help guide this decision.

Ease of use is often one of the most important considerations. Accounting systems should feel intuitive rather than overwhelming. Beginners benefit from software that offers clear instructions, simple interfaces, and helpful tutorials.

Scalability also matters. As a business grows, its financial management needs may become more complex. Choosing tools that can expand alongside the business helps avoid the need to switch systems later.

Integration with other business tools is another valuable feature. Many accounting platforms connect with payment processors, inventory systems, payroll services, and customer relationship management software. These integrations allow financial data to flow smoothly between different parts of the business.

Security should never be overlooked. Financial records contain sensitive information about revenue, expenses, and banking activity. Reliable accounting tools use encryption and secure data storage to protect this information.

Cost is another practical consideration. Some accounting systems charge monthly subscription fees, while others offer tiered pricing based on features or transaction volume. Business owners should evaluate whether the benefits provided justify the expense.

Choosing the right accounting tools does not require selecting the most advanced system available. Instead, the goal is to find software that matches the needs of the business while remaining easy to maintain and understand.

USING TECHNOLOGY TO SIMPLIFY FINANCIAL MANAGEMENT

Technology has the power to transform financial management from a complicated task into a manageable routine. When used effectively, digital tools help business owners stay organized, informed, and prepared.

One of the greatest advantages of modern accounting technology is accessibility. Financial information can be viewed from laptops, tablets, or smartphones. This allows business owners to monitor their financial position even while traveling or working remotely.

Real-time reporting provides another benefit. Instead of waiting until the end of the month to review financial results, entrepreneurs can check revenue trends and expense patterns at any time. This immediate visibility helps identify issues before they become serious problems.

Technology also improves communication with financial professionals. Accountants and bookkeepers can review digital records remotely, making collaboration faster and more efficient. Questions about transactions or financial reports can often be resolved quickly without exchanging physical documents.

Another important advantage is data organization. Digital accounting systems store financial information in structured formats that allow users to search, filter, and analyze transactions easily. This organization simplifies tasks such as tax preparation, financial planning, and performance analysis.

However, the true value of accounting technology lies not in the software itself but in the insights it provides. When financial information becomes easier to access and understand, business owners gain a clearer view of how their companies operate.

Technology cannot replace sound judgment or financial awareness. But when combined with a solid understanding of accounting principles, it becomes an invaluable partner in managing the financial health of a business.

By simplifying record keeping, improving accuracy, and providing real-time insights, modern accounting tools allow entrepreneurs and professionals to focus on what matters most—building stronger, more successful organizations.

CHAPTER 24

ACCOUNTING AND TAXES

Taxes are one of the few financial realities that every business eventually encounters. Whether someone runs a small freelance operation, manages a growing startup, or oversees a large organization, taxes become part of the financial landscape sooner or later. For many beginners, this area of business feels intimidating. Tax rules can appear complicated, deadlines can create pressure, and mistakes can be costly.

Accounting plays a central role in making the tax process manageable.

When financial records are accurate and well organized, preparing tax information becomes far less stressful. Income is already tracked, expenses are properly categorized, and supporting documentation is readily available. The numbers needed for tax reporting can often be pulled directly from financial statements.

Without proper accounting, the situation looks very different. Missing receipts, incomplete records, and disorganized financial data turn tax preparation into a time-consuming puzzle. Business owners may struggle to reconstruct their financial activity from memory or scattered bank statements.

Good accounting habits prevent this situation. By maintaining clear financial records throughout the year, businesses ensure that tax preparation becomes a straightforward step rather than a last-minute scramble.

Accounting also helps businesses understand their tax obligations more clearly. Taxes are generally calculated based on financial performance. When profit, expenses, and financial transactions are tracked properly, business owners can estimate their tax responsibilities and avoid unpleasant surprises.

Rather than viewing accounting and taxes as separate tasks, it is more helpful to see them as connected parts of the same financial system. Accounting records the story of the business. Taxes rely on that story to determine how much must be paid to government authorities.

When the story is organized and accurate, the tax process becomes far easier to navigate.

WHY ACCURATE FINANCIAL RECORDS MATTER FOR TAXES

Accurate financial records serve as the foundation for reliable tax reporting. Governments require businesses to report income and expenses honestly so that taxes can be calculated correctly. Accounting records provide the evidence that supports those calculations.

When revenue is recorded consistently throughout the year, the total income reported on tax forms reflects the true financial activity of the business. Similarly, when expenses are documented properly, businesses can claim legitimate deductions that reduce their taxable income.

Consider a freelance photographer who tracks all income from client projects and carefully records expenses for equipment, travel, and editing software. At tax time, the photographer can review the financial records and easily determine the total profit for the year. Because expenses are documented, those costs can be deducted appropriately.

Now imagine the same photographer without organized records. Income may be scattered across multiple payment platforms, while receipts for expenses are stored in different places or lost entirely.

Preparing tax information would require hours of searching through emails and bank statements, and some legitimate deductions might be missed.

Accurate records also provide protection in the event of a tax audit. Tax authorities sometimes request documentation to verify reported income and deductions. Businesses that maintain organized accounting records can respond confidently by providing the necessary evidence.

Without documentation, proving the legitimacy of certain expenses becomes much more difficult.

Beyond compliance, accurate financial records help business owners anticipate tax obligations. When financial statements show strong profits during the year, entrepreneurs can prepare for the taxes that will follow rather than being surprised when tax payments become due.

Clear accounting records transform tax preparation from a stressful obligation into a predictable process.

BASIC FINANCIAL DOCUMENTATION

Every financial transaction leaves a trail of documents that help verify what occurred. These documents form the backbone of accounting records and provide support for tax reporting.

Invoices are among the most important records for businesses that sell products or services. An invoice documents the amount charged to a customer, the date of the transaction, and the details of the goods or services provided. Keeping copies of invoices ensures that revenue records remain accurate.

Receipts provide evidence of expenses. Whenever a business purchases supplies, equipment, or services, the receipt confirms the cost and date of the transaction. Digital copies of receipts can be stored within accounting systems to simplify record keeping.

Bank statements also play a crucial role in financial documentation. They provide an official record of deposits, withdrawals, and transfers that occur within a business account. Many accountants use bank statements to verify that recorded transactions match the activity reported by the bank.

Contracts and agreements may also be important documentation. For example, service agreements with clients or lease agreements for office space help explain certain financial transactions that appear in accounting records.

Payroll records represent another category of documentation for businesses with employees. These records track wages, taxes withheld, and employer contributions, ensuring that compensation is reported accurately.

Maintaining organized documentation allows businesses to trace each financial entry back to its original source. This connection between transactions and documents strengthens the reliability of accounting records and simplifies the process of preparing financial reports.

When documentation is stored systematically—either digitally or in organized physical files—retrieving information later becomes far easier.

PREPARING FINANCIAL DATA FOR TAX REPORTING

As the end of the financial year approaches, businesses must organize their accounting information so that it can be used for tax reporting. This preparation often begins with reviewing financial records to ensure that transactions have been recorded accurately.

One important step involves reconciling accounts. Reconciliation means comparing accounting records with external documents such as bank statements. This process helps confirm that all transactions have been captured correctly and that account balances are accurate.

Next, businesses typically review their income and expense categories. Ensuring that transactions are properly classified helps produce financial statements that clearly reflect the company's financial activity.

For example, separating marketing expenses from office supplies allows business owners to understand how money is being spent while also ensuring that deductions are categorized correctly for tax purposes.

Financial statements such as the income statement and balance sheet play an important role during tax preparation. The income statement summarizes revenue and expenses for the year, revealing the profit figure that often forms the basis for calculating taxes.

The balance sheet provides additional context by showing assets, liabilities, and equity. While tax calculations focus primarily on income, the balance sheet helps confirm the accuracy of financial records.

Some businesses also review depreciation schedules for equipment and long-term assets. Depreciation spreads the cost of these assets over several years, which can influence how expenses appear in financial reports and tax calculations.

Preparing financial data in advance allows tax reporting to proceed smoothly. Instead of searching for missing information at the last minute, businesses can rely on organized accounting records that already contain the necessary details.

WORKING WITH ACCOUNTANTS AND TAX PROFESSIONALS

Even when business owners maintain strong accounting systems, many choose to work with accountants or tax professionals when preparing tax filings. These experts bring specialized knowledge that helps ensure compliance with tax regulations.

Accountants review financial records to verify accuracy and identify potential issues. They may recommend adjustments, suggest additional deductions, or clarify how certain transactions should be recorded.

Tax professionals also help interpret tax laws that affect businesses. Regulations may change over time, and professionals stay informed about these developments. Their guidance helps businesses avoid mistakes that could lead to penalties or missed opportunities.

Working with an accountant does not mean surrendering control of financial information. Instead, it often becomes a collaborative process. Business owners provide the financial data generated by their accounting systems, while professionals help translate that information into the correct tax reporting format.

Communication plays an important role in this relationship. When accountants understand the nature of a business's operations, they can offer more relevant advice. For example, they may suggest ways to structure expenses or plan purchases that align with tax regulations.

Many businesses also benefit from periodic consultations with accountants during the year rather than waiting until tax season. These conversations help ensure that financial decisions remain aligned with tax requirements.

By combining organized accounting records with professional guidance, businesses can navigate tax obligations with greater confidence.

AVOIDING TAX-RELATED FINANCIAL MISTAKES

Tax-related mistakes often arise from simple oversights rather than complex misunderstandings. Many problems can be prevented through consistent accounting practices and careful attention to detail.

One common issue occurs when businesses fail to separate personal and business finances. Mixing these transactions creates confusion about which expenses belong to the business and which do not. Maintaining separate bank accounts for business activity simplifies both accounting and tax reporting.

Another frequent mistake involves neglecting to record income from all sources. Businesses that receive payments through multiple platforms—such as bank transfers, online payment services, or credit card processors—must ensure that each source is included in their accounting records.

Incomplete expense tracking can also lead to problems. When legitimate business expenses are not recorded, the business may end up paying more tax than necessary because those costs were never deducted.

Late preparation is another common challenge. Waiting until the last moment to organize financial records increases the risk of errors and overlooked information. Regular record keeping throughout the year prevents this pressure from building.

Businesses should also remain mindful of important deadlines. Tax authorities often impose penalties for late filings or missed payments. Maintaining a clear calendar of financial obligations helps ensure that these deadlines are met.

Perhaps the most effective way to avoid tax mistakes is to treat accounting as an ongoing process rather than an annual task. When financial records are updated regularly and reviewed consistently, tax preparation becomes far simpler.

Accurate accounting provides a clear picture of the business's financial activity. With that clarity in place, tax reporting becomes a structured extension of the accounting system rather than a separate and stressful event.

CHAPTER 25

A COMPLETE ACCOUNTING EXAMPLE

Up to this point, the ideas of accounting have been introduced one piece at a time. Assets, liabilities, equity, journal entries, ledgers, trial balances, income statements, balance sheets, and cash flow statements have each had their turn. That approach makes learning easier, but real business life does not arrive in neatly separated lessons. In a real business, these pieces work together all at once.

That is why it helps to walk through a full example from start to finish.

A complete example turns accounting from something theoretical into something you can follow with your own eyes. You get to see how a business begins, how transactions are recorded, how the books build over time, and how those records eventually become financial statements. More importantly, you get to see how the numbers tell a story.

This kind of example is where many beginners finally relax a little. The subject stops feeling like scattered rules and starts feeling like a practical system. A sale affects cash or receivables. Expenses reduce profit. Assets grow when equipment is purchased. Liabilities increase when the business borrows. Equity changes as the owner invests money and the business earns profit. The logic becomes visible.

To keep the example clear, we will use a small service-based business rather than a large company with dozens of complicated accounts. The goal is not to overwhelm. The goal is to show how the accounting system works in a realistic but manageable setting.

Imagine a business that is new enough to be understandable, but active enough to show the key ideas in action. That is exactly what we are going to build.

SETTING UP A SIMPLE BUSINESS SCENARIO

Let us imagine a small business called **BrightStart Design Studio**. It is a one-owner graphic design business that creates logos, flyers, social media graphics, and simple branding materials for small companies.

This kind of business works well for a beginner example because it includes many of the transactions a new business might face:

- owner investment
- equipment purchase
- service revenue
- rent
- supplies
- payments from clients
- bills paid later
- ordinary monthly expenses

BrightStart Design Studio begins operations on January 1.

The owner, Ada, starts the business by investing personal savings into the company. She wants to keep the setup simple but professional, so she rents a small office, buys a computer and printer, opens a business bank account, and begins offering services to clients.

During the first month, the following transactions occur:

1. Ada invests $10,000 cash into the business.

2. The business buys a computer and printer for $2,500 cash.
3. The business pays $1,200 for one month's office rent.
4. The business buys office supplies on credit for $300.
5. The business earns $2,000 from a client and receives cash immediately.
6. The business completes another project worth $1,500 and agrees to collect payment later.
7. The business pays $200 for internet and software subscriptions.
8. The business pays $150 toward the office supplies bill.
9. The owner withdraws $500 cash for personal use.
10. The business receives $1,000 from the client who previously owed money.
11. The business pays $400 for advertising.

This is a modest month, but it is enough to show how accounting works in a full cycle.

Before recording anything, it helps to identify the accounts we are likely to use:

- Cash
- Accounts Receivable

- Office Supplies
- Equipment
- Accounts Payable
- Owner's Capital
- Owner's Drawings
- Service Revenue
- Rent Expense
- Internet and Software Expense
- Advertising Expense

That is already enough structure to support a working accounting system.

RECORDING TRANSACTIONS STEP-BY-STEP

Now let us record each transaction using simple journal entries and talk through the logic behind them.

Transaction 1: Owner invests $10,000 cash into the business

The business receives cash, so the cash account increases. The owner's investment increases equity.

Journal Entry
Debit Cash $10,000
Credit Owner's Capital $10,000

This entry records the starting financial foundation of the business.

Transaction 2: Business buys a computer and printer for $2,500 cash

The business gains equipment, which is an asset. Cash decreases because the purchase is paid immediately.

Journal Entry
Debit Equipment $2,500
Credit Cash $2,500

This does not create an expense right away because the equipment is a long-term asset.

Transaction 3: Business pays $1,200 for one month's office rent

This is a normal operating cost for the month, so rent expense increases. Cash decreases.

Journal Entry
Debit Rent Expense $1,200
Credit Cash $1,200

Transaction 4: Business buys office supplies on credit for $300

The business receives supplies, which increase assets. Because payment will come later, a liability is created.

Journal Entry
Debit Office Supplies $300
Credit Accounts Payable $300

Transaction 5: Business earns $2,000 from a client and receives cash immediately

Cash increases because the customer pays now. Revenue increases because the business earned income.

Journal Entry
Debit Cash $2,000
Credit Service Revenue $2,000

Transaction 6: Business completes another project worth $1,500 and will be paid later

The business has earned revenue, but cash has not arrived yet. Instead, the business records an asset called accounts receivable.

Journal Entry
Debit Accounts Receivable $1,500
Credit Service Revenue $1,500

This is a good reminder that revenue can be recognized before cash is received.

Transaction 7: Business pays $200 for internet and software subscriptions

This is a monthly operating expense, so expense increases and cash decreases.

Journal Entry
Debit Internet and Software Expense $200
Credit Cash $200

Transaction 8: Business pays $150 toward the office supplies bill

The business reduces what it owes to the supplier, so accounts payable decreases. Cash decreases because money is paid.

Journal Entry
Debit Accounts Payable $150
Credit Cash $150

Transaction 9: Owner withdraws $500 cash for personal use

This is not a business expense. It is a withdrawal by the owner, so drawings increase and cash decreases.

Journal Entry
Debit Owner's Drawings $500
Credit Cash $500

This distinction matters. If the withdrawal were recorded as an expense, profit would be distorted.

Transaction 10: Business receives $1,000 from the client who previously owed money

Cash increases because payment is received. Accounts receivable decreases because the customer now owes less.

Journal Entry
Debit Cash $1,000
Credit Accounts Receivable $1,000

Transaction 11: Business pays $400 for advertising

Advertising is an operating expense, so that account increases. Cash decreases.

Journal Entry
Debit Advertising Expense $400
Credit Cash $400

Now let us summarize the effect of these entries in a simple account balance view.

Cash

Starting from zero:

- +10,000 owner investment
- -2,500 equipment purchase
- -1,200 rent
- +2,000 cash service revenue
- -200 internet/software
- -150 payment to supplier
- -500 owner withdrawal
- +1,000 collection from customer
- -400 advertising

Ending cash balance = **$8,050**

Accounts Receivable

- +1,500 revenue earned on credit
- -1,000 collected from customer

Ending accounts receivable = **$500**

Office Supplies

- +300 supplies purchased

Ending office supplies = **$300**

Equipment

- +2,500 purchased

Ending equipment = **$2,500**

Accounts Payable

- +300 supplies bought on credit
- -150 payment to supplier

Ending accounts payable = **$150**

Owner's Capital

- +10,000 investment

Ending owner's capital = **$10,000**

Owner's Drawings

- +500 withdrawal

Ending drawings = **$500**

Service Revenue

- +2,000 cash service
- +1,500 credit service

Ending service revenue = **$3,500**

Expenses

- Rent Expense = $1,200
- Internet and Software Expense = $200
- Advertising Expense = $400

Total expenses = **$1,800**

At this point, the accounting records already tell a useful story. The business earned revenue, managed several expenses, bought equipment, and still ended the month with a solid cash balance.

PREPARING FINANCIAL STATEMENTS

Now let us turn those records into the three main financial statements.

Income Statement

The income statement focuses on performance for the month.

BrightStart Design Studio
Income Statement
For the Month Ended January 31

Service Revenue $3,500

Expenses:
Rent Expense $1,200
Internet and Software Expense 200
Advertising Expense 400

Total Expenses $1,800

Net Income $1,700

This report tells us that the business earned $1,700 in profit during its first month.

That is a healthy sign for a new business. It means the business did more than stay busy. It produced a positive financial result after covering its expenses.

Statement of Owner's Equity

Now let us show how equity changed during the month.

BrightStart Design Studio
Statement of Owner's Equity
For the Month Ended January 31

Owner's Capital, beginning $0
Add: Owner Investment 10,000
Add: Net Income 1,700
Less: Owner Drawings .... (500)

Owner's Capital, ending $11,200

This report connects the income statement to the balance sheet. The $1,700 profit increased owner's equity, while the $500 withdrawal reduced it.

Balance Sheet

Now let us prepare the balance sheet at January 31.

BrightStart Design Studio
Balance Sheet
January 31

Assets
Cash $8,050
Accounts Receivable 500
Office Supplies 300
Equipment 2,500

Total Assets **$11,350**

Liabilities

Accounts Payable $150

Total Liabilities **$150**

Owner's Equity

Owner's Capital 11,200

Total Owner's Equity **$11,200**

Total Liabilities and Owner's Equity $11,350

The statement balances, which is exactly what we want:

Assets = Liabilities + Equity
$11,350 = $150 + $11,200

That confirms the accounting equation is being respected.

Simple Cash Flow View

Although not all beginner books prepare a full formal cash flow statement in the first complete example, it helps to show the basic movement of cash.

Cash	**Inflows**
Owner investment	$10,000
Cash from client	2,000
Collection from receivable	1,000
Total Cash Inflows	**$13,000**

Cash	**Outflows**
Equipment purchase	$2,500
Rent	1,200
Internet/software	200
Supplier payment	150
Owner withdrawal	500
Advertising	400
Total Cash Outflows	**$4,950**

Net Increase in Cash	**$8,050**

Because the business started with zero cash, the ending cash balance is also $8,050.

This cash view helps make a key point: the business earned $1,700 in profit, but its cash increased by much more than that because of the owner's investment and customer collections. That is exactly why profit and cash should never be treated as the same thing.

INTERPRETING THE FINANCIAL RESULTS

Now that the statements are prepared, the next step is interpretation. This is where accounting becomes truly useful.

The income statement shows a first-month profit of $1,700. That suggests the business's services are being priced high enough to cover current operating expenses. For a new design studio, that is encouraging. It means the business is not simply generating activity. It is creating value.

The balance sheet shows total assets of $11,350, with only $150 in liabilities. That means the business is lightly burdened by debt at this stage. Most of its resources are financed by the owner's investment and the profit already earned. That gives the business a stable starting position.

The cash balance of $8,050 is also strong. This matters because new businesses often feel pressure in the early months. Cash gives flexibility. It allows the owner to handle future expenses, buy more tools if needed, or survive a slower month without immediate panic.

Accounts receivable stands at $500. That is not a problem by itself, but it is worth watching. The business has already learned one early lesson of accounting: not every sale becomes cash immediately. If receivables begin to grow too much in future months, cash flow could become tighter even if revenue stays strong.

Accounts payable is only $150, which means the business does not owe much at the moment. That reduces short-term pressure.

The owner's ending equity of $11,200 is another positive sign. It shows that the combination of owner investment and retained profit has built a solid foundation in a short time.

But the most useful interpretation goes beyond just calling the month "good" or "bad." A thoughtful owner might ask:

- Can this level of revenue be repeated next month?
- Are the current expenses typical, or were some unusually low?
- Will advertising continue at this level, and is it bringing in enough work?
- Should the business begin budgeting for taxes or future equipment upgrades?

- How quickly are customers paying, and should payment terms be tightened?

Those are the kinds of questions accounting should lead to.

Now imagine a different outcome. Suppose the business had earned strong revenue but still had very little cash. Or suppose expenses were much higher, leaving almost no profit. The same accounting process would still work, but the interpretation would change. That is the beauty of financial statements. They do not flatter. They reveal.

LESSONS FROM THE EXAMPLE

A complete example like this leaves behind several useful lessons.

The first is that accounting is not random. Every transaction has a place, and every place tells part of the financial story. Owner investment, customer payments, unpaid invoices, expenses, withdrawals, and bills all flow through the system in ways that can be tracked and understood.

The second lesson is that the accounting equation is not just theory. It is active in every step of the process. When assets rise, something else changes too. When the books are recorded properly, the final balance sheet proves that the equation still holds.

The third lesson is that profit does not tell the entire story. BrightStart Design Studio earned $1,700 in net income, but the cash position, receivables, liabilities, and owner withdrawals all added extra layers of meaning. That is why reading only the income statement is never enough.

The fourth lesson is that financial statements are connected. Revenue and expenses created net income. Net income affected owner's equity. Cash movements helped explain the real financial position. The reports worked together as a system.

The fifth lesson is that even a simple business can benefit from proper accounting. BrightStart Design Studio is not a giant company. It is a small service business. Still, accounting gave the owner a clear picture of performance, stability, and financial direction. That is exactly why accounting matters for beginners, freelancers, and small business owners, not just for large corporations.

There is also a practical lesson in discipline. None of these statements could have been prepared accurately if the transactions had not been recorded carefully. Good accounting does not begin with fancy reports. It begins with ordinary consistency.

Finally, this example shows something many beginners need to hear: accounting becomes much less intimidating once the pieces are seen working together. What felt separate before now starts to feel connected. Transactions create records. Records create balances. Balances create reports. Reports create insight.

That is the full cycle.

And once that cycle makes sense, accounting stops feeling like a wall of rules and starts feeling like a way to understand what a business is truly doing.

CHAPTER 26

KEY ACCOUNTING PRINCIPLES TO REMEMBER

There comes a point in learning accounting where the subject stops feeling like a pile of terms and starts feeling more like common sense with structure. That shift matters. It is the difference between memorizing words and actually knowing what you are looking at when you open a financial report.

By now, the bigger picture should feel more familiar. A business earns money, spends money, owns things, owes things, and keeps records so none of it turns into guesswork. The details matter, but the heart of accounting is not mystery. It is order. It is a way of keeping score honestly.

A small business owner may not need to speak like an accountant. A freelancer may never use every technical term in a formal meeting. A student may still be learning the rhythm of debits and credits. But anyone who understands the key principles can make better decisions, ask better questions, and avoid being misled by numbers that look impressive but say very little on their own.

This part of the journey is less about introducing something brand new and more about settling the important ideas into place. What are the principles worth holding onto when the details get messy? What habits keep the books useful instead of confusing? What mindset helps a beginner grow into someone who can read numbers without feeling lost?

Those are the ideas that matter here.

CORE ACCOUNTING CONCEPTS RECAP

At the center of accounting is a very simple truth: every business has a financial story, and that story can be recorded clearly or poorly. Accounting is the system that decides which one it will be.

One of the most important ideas to hold onto is the difference between **activity** and **results**. A business can be busy without being profitable. It can have customers, invoices, orders, and movement everywhere, but still be weak underneath. That is why accounting does not stop at "money came in." It also asks what it cost to earn that money, what remains, and what obligations are still hanging in the background.

Then there is the accounting equation:

Assets = Liabilities + Equity

This is not just a classroom formula. It is the frame holding the whole subject together. Assets are what the business has. Liabilities are what it owes. Equity is what belongs to the owner after debts are taken into account. Every recorded transaction fits somewhere inside that structure. If the numbers do not respect that relationship, something has gone wrong.

Another essential idea is that **not all financial events are about cash**. This is where beginners often stumble. A sale can happen before payment arrives. An expense can exist before the bill is paid. Equipment can be bought once and used for years. Cash matters deeply, but cash alone does not tell the whole story. That is why accounting separates profit from cash flow and gives each its proper place.

It also helps to remember the role of the three core financial statements.

The **income statement** answers one broad question: did the business earn more than it spent during the period?

The **balance sheet** answers another: what does the business own and owe right now?

The **cash flow statement** answers a question that often feels the most urgent in real life: where did the money actually go, and where did it come from?

Each report matters. None of them should be treated like the only one that counts.

There is also a deeper concept running quietly underneath all of this: **timing**. Good accounting puts income and expenses in the periods where they truly belong. That is why adjustments matter. That is why prepaid items, accrued expenses, and receivables are worth understanding. Without proper timing, the books can be technically neat while financially misleading.

One more concept deserves to stay close to the surface: **classification matters**. Recording a transaction is not enough. It needs to be recorded in the right place. A loan is not revenue. An owner withdrawal is not an expense. Equipment is not the same as office supplies.

These distinctions may seem small until the reports start telling the wrong story because of them.

If all of this is reduced to its simplest form, the core accounting concepts sound something like this:

Money moving is not the same as profit.
Profit is not the same as cash.
A business can look healthy and still be under pressure.
A business can look ordinary and still be financially strong.
The reports only become useful when the records underneath them are honest and well organized.

That is the ground everything else stands on.

ESSENTIAL FINANCIAL RULES FOR BEGINNERS

Beginners often look for rules because rules feel safer than interpretation. That instinct is understandable. When the subject still feels unfamiliar, a few steady principles can prevent a lot of unnecessary confusion.

One rule worth remembering is this: **record transactions when they happen, not when you finally feel like dealing with them**. Delay creates distortion.

Small things get forgotten first, and small things add up faster than people expect. A business owner who waits three weeks to record expenses is not saving time. They are creating a fog that will have to be cleared later.

Another rule: **separate business money from personal money**. This sounds basic, but it quietly solves dozens of future problems. When personal spending and business spending mix together, the numbers lose their shape. Profit becomes harder to measure. Expenses become harder to defend. Tax preparation becomes harder than it needs to be. Clear boundaries produce cleaner records.

A third rule: **never assume revenue means success**. Sales can flatter a weak business. Strong top-line numbers can hide weak margins, rising costs, unpaid customer balances, or poor cash flow. Revenue deserves attention, but it should never be admired without asking what was required to produce it.

Another practical rule is to **treat cash like oxygen, not decoration**. Some beginners think of cash as one number among many. In real business life, it often decides how calm or chaotic the month will feel. A profitable business with no cash breathing room can become desperate very quickly. Watching cash is not pessimism. It is basic survival.

It also helps to remember that **every number invites a second question**. If revenue grew, ask why. If profit dropped, ask what changed. If expenses increased, ask whether the increase was useful, wasteful, temporary, or structural. Financial reports should not stop thought. They should provoke it.

Here is another rule that saves people from trouble: **do not guess when a proper category matters**. If something is unclear, slow down and work out what the transaction actually is. Is it an expense, an asset, a liability, or an owner transaction? Guessing carelessly may save a minute now and cost hours later.

One more useful rule: **review your numbers regularly, even when nothing seems wrong**. Waiting until a crisis appears is like checking your brakes only after the car starts sliding. Regular review keeps the business familiar. It lets unusual changes stand out quickly. When people know their normal patterns, they spot trouble earlier.

And then there is a rule that belongs more to judgment than bookkeeping: **do not let one good month make you careless, and do not let one bad month**

make you dramatic. Accounting becomes most useful when numbers are read in context. Trends matter more than emotional reactions. One month may reflect timing, seasonality, or unusual costs. Patterns tell the deeper truth.

The most grounded beginners are usually the ones who learn these habits early. They do not try to sound impressive. They simply keep the numbers clean, stay curious, and resist the temptation to treat accounting like something that can be tidied up later.

BEST PRACTICES FOR FINANCIAL RECORD KEEPING

Good record keeping rarely feels glamorous, but bad record keeping has a talent for becoming memorable in all the wrong ways.

A missing invoice may not seem serious until a payment dispute appears. A lost receipt may not matter until tax time. A few uncategorized transactions may feel harmless until the income statement starts making less and less sense. The damage from weak record keeping is often delayed, which is why so many people underestimate it at first.

Strong financial records usually come from simple habits done consistently.

One of the best practices is to **record close to the source**. When a transaction happens, deal with it while the memory is still fresh and the supporting document is easy to find. The longer a transaction sits unrecorded, the more likely it is to be forgotten, mislabeled, or misunderstood later.

Another good habit is to **keep supporting documents organized in a way your future self will appreciate**. This can be digital, physical, or both. The method matters less than the logic. If a purchase, payment, or invoice needs to be verified later, there should be a clear trail leading back to it.

Consistency matters more than perfection. A business owner does not need a beautiful filing system that collapses after two weeks. A plain, workable system that gets used regularly is far better. The real question is simple: if you needed proof or clarification later, could you find it without stress?

It also helps to **use clear account categories and stick with them**. When expenses are categorized differently every month, comparisons become muddy. If advertising is recorded under marketing in January, promotion in February, and miscellaneous in March, the reports lose their usefulness. The point of categories is not decoration. It is clarity over time.

Reconciliation is another habit worth respecting. Bank records should not live in a separate universe from the books. Regularly matching accounting records to bank activity helps catch errors, missed entries, duplicates, or odd transactions before they become harder to untangle.

There is also value in leaving useful notes where they matter. Not every transaction needs a long explanation, but some do. A short note about what a payment was for, why an unusual entry exists, or how a figure was calculated can save a surprising amount of time later.

One of the most overlooked best practices is to **close each period with intention**. Do not let one month bleed lazily into the next. Review what belongs in that period, what still needs adjustment, and whether the balances make sense. This is especially important for businesses with unpaid invoices, advance payments, or recurring expenses.

And perhaps most important of all, treat record keeping as part of running the business, not as an interruption from it. The numbers are not outside the business. They are one of the clearest expressions of how the business is actually doing.

A business with clean records has options. It can prepare reports faster, apply for funding more confidently, work with professionals more smoothly, and make decisions with less hesitation. A business with messy records may still survive, but it usually does so with more stress than necessary.

BUILDING LONG-TERM FINANCIAL CONFIDENCE

Financial confidence does not arrive all at once. It builds in layers.

At first, confidence may simply mean not panicking when you see an income statement. Later, it may mean understanding why profit and cash do not match. Later still, it may mean noticing a worrying pattern early, asking better questions, or making a decision based on evidence instead of anxiety.

That kind of confidence is different from arrogance. It does not mean pretending to know everything. It means becoming steady enough with the basics that the numbers no longer feel like a threat.

For many beginners, confidence grows through repetition. The more often you read reports, record transactions, review balances, and connect the statements to real business activity, the more natural the subject becomes. Familiarity softens fear. Patterns emerge. Confusion gives way to recognition.

Confidence also grows when you stop expecting accounting to be dramatic. Most of the time, it is not. It is routine. It is patient work. It is checking, recording, reviewing, and asking sensible questions. That may sound plain, but plain habits are often what create strong businesses.

Another part of long-term confidence is knowing when to slow down. Not every financial issue should be handled with immediate certainty. Some situations deserve a second look, a reconciliation, or professional advice. Real confidence includes humility. It knows the difference between understanding enough to act and pretending enough to feel clever.

There is also a mindset shift that matters here. A lot of beginners secretly treat accounting like a test they hope to pass and leave behind. That approach keeps the subject feeling stiff. It helps more to treat accounting as an ongoing tool for seeing clearly. When that happens, the work feels less like performance and more like orientation. You are not trying to impress anyone. You are trying to know where the business stands.

Picture a small business owner five years into the future. They may still not love every bookkeeping task. But they know what rising receivables suggest. They know the difference between busy and profitable. They can look at a balance sheet and understand what is tight, what is stable, and what needs attention. They ask sharper questions. They make fewer avoidable mistakes. They do not feel financially blind anymore.

That is what long-term confidence looks like.

It is built from understanding the principles, respecting the records, reading the reports, and staying close enough to the numbers that nothing important becomes a surprise for too long.

And once that confidence settles in, accounting stops feeling like a foreign subject you visit under pressure. It starts feeling like part of the way you run a business with honesty, awareness, and control.

CHAPTER 27

YOUR NEXT STEPS IN FINANCIAL LEARNING

Learning accounting is a bit like learning to read weather signs after years of simply walking under the sky. At first, everything looks like a blur of numbers, labels, and formal reports. Then something changes. You begin to notice patterns. You see where pressure is building. You recognize when things are healthy, when something is off, and when a business is only pretending to be stronger than it really is.

That shift matters.

The real value of financial learning is not that it makes someone sound more knowledgeable in a meeting. It is that it changes the quality of their decisions. A person who understands accounting no longer has to rely entirely on instinct, hope, or surface impressions. They have something firmer to stand on. They can look at the numbers and make sense of what is happening underneath the noise.

But learning does not end once the basic terms, reports, and principles are familiar. In many ways, that is where the more useful part begins. Once the foundation is in place, accounting starts showing up in real life everywhere. It appears in pricing decisions, client work, pay negotiations, side businesses, budgeting conversations, loan applications, tax preparation, inventory choices, hiring plans, and growth opportunities.

This is where the subject becomes practical.

You do not have to become an accountant to benefit deeply from accounting knowledge. You simply need to use it often enough that it becomes part of how you think. That is how confidence is built. Not through memorizing more terms than anyone else in the room, but through repeated contact with real business numbers until the subject feels less foreign and more useful.

The next stage is about applying what you know, staying curious, and continuing to sharpen the habit of financial awareness.

APPLYING ACCOUNTING KNOWLEDGE IN REAL LIFE

Accounting becomes more valuable the moment it leaves the page and starts influencing real choices.

A reader may understand the income statement in theory, but the lesson deepens when they use it to look at a real business and ask, "Are we actually making enough after costs?" The balance sheet becomes more meaningful when it helps someone notice that a business owns useful assets but is carrying more short-term pressure than expected. Cash flow becomes much clearer when a person sees firsthand how delayed customer payments can create stress even during a profitable period.

This is where financial learning matures. The subject stops being about definitions and starts becoming a lens.

Take a simple real-life example. A freelance writer has several regular clients and feels reasonably busy each month. Before learning accounting, they may judge success mainly by how full the calendar feels. After learning accounting, they begin tracking revenue by client, software expenses, internet costs, marketing costs, and taxes set aside. Very quickly, a different kind of clarity appears. Some clients are profitable and easy to manage. Others take too much time for too little return. What looked like a full business begins to divide itself into strong work and weak work.

That is accounting in real life.

Or consider a small fashion retailer deciding whether to order more stock. Without accounting knowledge, the owner might think only about demand and excitement. With accounting knowledge, the owner asks sharper questions. How quickly does this inventory usually move? How much cash will this tie up? What are the current margins? Are there other obligations due this month that make a large purchase risky right now? The decision becomes more disciplined, not more fearful.

The same applies in workplaces. A manager who understands accounting can contribute more meaningfully to budgeting discussions, staffing decisions, pricing questions, or performance reviews. Instead of simply saying a project "seems expensive," they can discuss margins, overhead, cash impact, or return on spending with greater confidence.

Even outside formal business settings, accounting knowledge improves judgment. It helps people understand the difference between owning an asset and carrying a liability, between growth and overextension, between income and usable cash. These are not narrow bookkeeping ideas. They are practical financial habits.

One of the best ways to apply accounting knowledge is to start with something close and manageable. That could be a small side hustle, a freelance business, a family shop, a personal project, or a case study from a company you admire. Look at the money coming in. Look at the money going out. Group it honestly. Watch what happens over a month or two. You do not need a giant enterprise to begin thinking clearly.

The point is not to turn every decision into a spreadsheet exercise. The point is to use accounting often enough that it starts strengthening everyday judgment.

CONTINUING YOUR FINANCIAL EDUCATION

A beginner who understands the foundations of accounting has already crossed an important line. The subject is no longer completely unfamiliar. That matters. But strong financial understanding grows through continued exposure, not a single round of learning.

The next step is not necessarily to study harder in a formal sense. It is to study more usefully.

Some people continue by reading more advanced material on bookkeeping, financial analysis, managerial accounting, or small business finance. Others learn by reviewing actual financial statements from companies, studying how different industries operate, or using accounting software with real examples. Both approaches can work. What matters most is staying connected to real financial situations rather than drifting back into vague theory.

It helps to choose the next learning step based on your life, not someone else's idea of what sounds impressive.

A student planning to work in business might explore ratio analysis, budgeting, or business valuation.

A small business owner might go deeper into cash forecasting, inventory control, payroll basics, and tax planning.

A freelancer might focus on pricing, expense tracking, profit planning, and separating personal from business finances.

A manager might need stronger confidence reading internal reports, evaluating department budgets, or discussing performance metrics.

Financial education becomes more powerful when it follows relevance.

One practical way to keep learning is to review actual reports regularly. This does not need to be formal or heavy. Even something as simple as reading one income statement carefully each month and asking what stands out can sharpen understanding over time. Patterns begin to feel more familiar. Weak spots become easier to notice. Good questions come faster.

Another useful path is learning how technology supports the process. Accounting software, dashboards, invoicing systems, and reporting tools do not replace understanding, but they do shape how modern financial work gets done. Becoming comfortable with those tools makes the knowledge more usable.

It is also worth learning how accounting connects to related subjects. Budgeting, finance, tax planning, pricing strategy, operations, and business growth decisions all become easier to understand when accounting sits in the background. In that sense, financial education does not branch away from accounting. It branches out through it.

One warning is worth mentioning here: avoid the trap of endless passive learning. Reading ten more explanations without applying any of them often creates the illusion of progress without much real growth. Better to learn one concept and use it than to skim fifty and retain none.

Real financial education often looks ordinary from the outside. It looks like checking reports, asking questions, reviewing decisions, learning from mistakes, and staying curious about how the numbers connect to reality. That kind of learning lasts longer than cramming definitions ever will.

DEVELOPING FINANCIAL AWARENESS

Financial awareness is more than accounting knowledge. It is the habit of noticing what the numbers are quietly saying before the situation becomes urgent.

Some people only pay attention to finances when something feels wrong. Cash gets tight, profit drops, taxes loom, debt rises, or a major expense suddenly becomes difficult to handle. By then, the numbers are no longer offering gentle guidance. They are raising their voice.

Financial awareness prevents that kind of late surprise.

It develops when people stay close enough to their financial information that changes do not go unnoticed for long. That could mean reviewing monthly reports. It could mean watching cash balances with more intention. It could mean comparing actual results to expectations instead of just hoping things are fine.

A financially aware person tends to notice things earlier. They notice when revenue is climbing but cash is not. They notice when one expense category is slowly growing out of proportion. They notice when customer payments are arriving later than usual. They notice when the business feels busy but margins are quietly thinning.

That awareness is not paranoia. It is attentiveness.

Think of financial awareness like noticing the way a building sounds. Someone unfamiliar may not hear anything unusual. Someone who knows the structure well may notice a new creak, a subtle shift, or a small leak before real damage appears. Numbers behave the same way. When you know what is normal, unusual movement becomes easier to spot.

Developing that awareness often begins with simple repetition. Review the same types of reports regularly enough, and they stop feeling cold or abstract. They begin to feel familiar. You start noticing the story inside the figures instead of merely scanning totals.

A business owner might notice that sales always dip slightly after a certain period and prepare for it instead of panicking. A freelancer might realize that one quarter always carries heavier tax pressure and start setting money aside earlier. A manager might notice that a team is overspending in one category while underusing another. These are not dramatic discoveries. They are examples of financial awareness doing its work quietly and well.

It also helps to train yourself to ask a few recurring questions:

What changed?
Why did it change?
Was that change expected?
Is it temporary or part of a pattern?

What does this mean for the next few weeks or months?

Those questions build awareness faster than staring at numbers without direction.

Financial awareness also includes emotional balance. Numbers can trigger excitement, fear, pride, denial, or overreaction. A good month can make people careless. A rough month can make them pessimistic too quickly. Awareness means staying grounded enough to read the numbers honestly without handing them full control of your mood.

That balance matters. It keeps decision-making clearer. It helps a person respond to facts without turning every fluctuation into a crisis or a celebration.

BUILDING CONFIDENCE WITH BUSINESS NUMBERS

Many people do not actually hate numbers. What they hate is the feeling of not understanding them.

That feeling can be sharp. It shows up in meetings when financial terms are used too quickly. It shows up when reading reports that seem full of meaning for everyone else. It shows up when making business decisions and secretly wondering whether something important is being missed.

Confidence with business numbers is built by reducing that gap between what you see and what you understand.

The first step is accepting that confidence rarely arrives before practice. It usually arrives because of it. The people who seem calm around financial reports are often not magically gifted. They have simply spent enough time with the material that the patterns no longer feel threatening.

Confidence grows when you can look at a number and place it in context. Revenue means more when you connect it to cost. Profit means more when you compare it to cash flow. A healthy cash balance means more when you compare it to upcoming obligations. A high expense means more when you know whether it is producing return.

That is what turns isolated numbers into meaningful information.

One useful way to build confidence is to stop treating every report as something that must be understood all at once. Start smaller. Read one section carefully.

Follow one figure from one statement to another. Notice how net income affects equity. Notice how unpaid customer invoices affect cash. Notice how debt changes the shape of the balance sheet. Confidence builds through connection, not speed.

Another useful habit is speaking the numbers back in plain language. If revenue increased, say what that means in everyday terms. If liabilities rose, explain why that matters. If expenses grew faster than sales, describe the pressure clearly without hiding behind jargon. When you can translate business numbers into plain speech, understanding gets stronger.

It also helps to spend time with real examples instead of only polished explanations. Actual financial situations are messier, but they are more useful. A business with strong sales and weak cash. A company growing too quickly. A freelancer earning well but underpricing one major service. A shop with good margins but slow-moving stock. These situations develop judgment, not just recall.

Confidence grows faster when mistakes are treated as part of the process rather than proof of failure. Misreading a report once or asking a basic question is not a sign that you are bad with numbers. It is part of becoming better with them. The people who grow most are often the ones willing to revisit the basics without embarrassment.

Over time, confidence with business numbers starts to show up in practical ways. You ask sharper questions. You spot weak explanations more quickly. You become less impressed by big revenue figures that hide poor margins. You become less intimidated by formal reports. You do not need every number explained to you from the beginning each time.

That kind of confidence is deeply useful.

It helps in business. It helps in work. It helps when dealing with accountants, partners, clients, lenders, and even your own decisions. Most of all, it reduces the feeling of operating in the dark.

And that may be one of the most valuable outcomes of learning accounting well: not just knowing more terms, but becoming the kind of person who can look at the financial side of things and not immediately feel lost.

www.ingramcontent.com/pod-product-compliance
Lightning Source LLC
LaVergne TN
LVHW052218200926
848481LV00001B/143
9798330607402